MW01236266

A Pocket Guide to

Maui's Hāna Highway:
A VISITOR'S GUIDE
COMPLETELY REVISED EDITION

The winding highway from Waikamoi Ridge

by

Angela Kay Kepler

MUTUAL PUBLISHING

ISBN 1-56647-665-8
Library of Congress Catalog
Card Number 2004102122

First Printing, May 2004
Second Printing, March 2005
2 3 4 5 6 7 8 9

Design by Angela Wu-Ki

All photos by Angela Kay Kepler
unless otherwise noted

Mutual Publishing, LLC
1215 Center Street, Suite 210
Honolulu, Hawai'i 96816
Ph: (808) 732-1709
Fax: (808) 734-4094
mutual@mutualpublishing.com
www.mutualpublishing.com

Printed in Korea

Ho'okipa Beach, world-renowned surfing break

TABLE OF CONTENTS

Resembling cluster of porcelain shells,
shell ginger *(Alpinia zerumbet)* adorns
sections of the road.

ACKNOWLEDGMENTS

I wish to express my thanks to the many friends, colleagues and family who, over the past 25 years, accompanied me along, above or below the Hāna Highway: we shared tents, pouring rain, biting winds, pesty mosquitoes, scorching sun, squashed sandwiches, dwindling water supplies and precious morsels of chocolate. Their different eyes and perspectives expanded my vision, refreshing my enthusiasm for Maui's beauty. Special gratitude is extended to members of the Sierra and Mauna Ala Hiking Clubs, U.S. Fish & Wildlife and National Park Services. Tom Hauptman—helicopter pilot *par excellence*—plucked me from many remote locations in his helicopter, often under perilous flying conditions.

I lovingly acknowledge the early training from my parents and teachers, and the good behavior of my children, Sylvelin and Leilani. Cameron Kepler helped provide opportunities for fieldwork in areas difficult of access, proofread the original manuscript, and kindly allowed me to use several transparencies.

I gratefully acknowledge additional photos from David Boynton, Alan Bradbury, Bob Butterfield, Bob Hobdy, Ron Nagata/Haleakalā National Park Service and Stewart Pinsky.

Frank Rust, my husband, provided abundant love, cooperation, and encouragement in all aspects of this new version of a 20-year-old book.

To all, *mahalo pumehana* (my heartfelt thanks).

PREFACE

In a similar manner to the way in which concert program notes enhance one's appreciation of music, this book is intended to enrich one's experience of the noted drive to Hāna. Essentially a picture book, it is divided into 13 chapters, each corresponding to a variable length of road (see map). Although not exhaustive, I hope it will answer questions relating to plants, birds, mammals, geology, weather, Hawaiian culture and conservation of natural resources. You can identify sights and flowers along the way, and most importantly, enjoy the drive even if you never reach Hāna.

The road began as a rough track, way back in 1926, hacked out with sweat and tears by a prison gang. In 1934 and 1962, further improvements were made, including entirely new road sections (a few remnants of the "old highway" still exist). When tourism expanded on Maui (1980s), major improvements began, continuing to the present day.

Today, many concerned citizens are battling to designate this magnificent coastal road as a National Heritage Corridor. A twisting, narrow, mountain highway, it is an end in itself. It is not a road to be whizzed around hastily to reach a "vacation" destination. Stop frequently. Drive leisurely. Allow windward Maui's expansive views, colors, smells and sounds seep into you. They all contribute to a collective ambience.

Relish the continual flow of audio-visual beauty along the Hāna Highway as you would enjoy the progression of your favorite music as it weaves, moment by moment, through space.

(OPPISITE PAGE)
'Richmond Red,' an upright
heliconia *(Heliconia bihai X caribaea cv. 'Richmond Red')*

'Dwarf Chinese' banana, of low stature and common in Hāna Highway gardens.

DOS AND DON'TS ON THE HĀNA HIGHWAY

PLEASE DOS

- Be considerate of fellow travelers and respond to every "Yield" and "One-way Bridge" sign.

- Fill up with gasoline in Kahului or Pā'ia. There are no service stations until you reach Hāna.

- Take food and drink, although snacks are available en route. Numerous roadside fruit stands provide the tastiest, freshest, Maui-grown produce that you'll experience on the island.

- Take a raincoat and plastic bags for cameras.

- Watch children closely. The ground is generally muddy, the rocks slippery, and many cliffs (that you may well be tempted to photograph views from) are deceptively dangerous.

PLEASE DON'TS

- Drive fast. Parts of the highway are extremely narrow and cliffy.

- Drink water from roadsides or streams. Upslope are either pig-infested forests or cow pastures.

- Dive into pools.

- Swim in the ocean at Kīpahulu.

- Walk away from the road unless along established trails. All land is private, requiring prior permission.

- Let children play on rock walls. Most are ancient and/or have special significance to Hawaiians. Please also do not erect your "own" stone altars. This is offensive to native Hawaiian people.

- Drive rental cars beyond Kīpahulu (jeeps are fine IF the road is open).

DRIVING TIMES TO HĀNA CHART (an unrushed pace)

FROM	TO	TIME
Kāanapali	Pā'ia	1 hour
Kīhei	Pā'ia	0 minutes
Pā'ia	Hāna	3 hours
Hāna	Kīpahulu (Haleakalā National Park)	1 hour

Map of East Maui

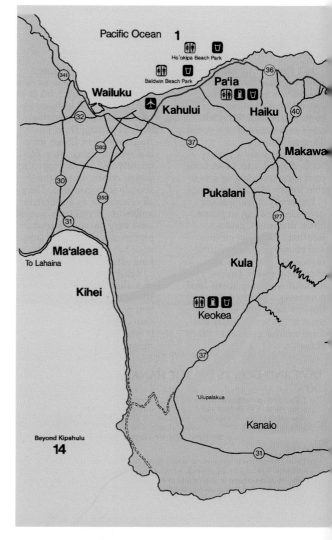

HANA HIGHWAY MAP

Miles 0 1 2 3 4   Kilometers 0 1 2 3 4

SYMBOLS

🔺 Tent

🚻 Toilet

⛽ Gas

💧 Drinking Water

— Hana Highway

— Other Roads

- - - - 4-Wheel Drive

Huelo

Kailua

3

4 5 6

7

Waikamoi

Puohokamoa

Kaumahina

Honomanu

Honomanu Bay

Ke'anae

Ke'anae Peninsula

Pauwelu Point

8

Wailua

9

Pua'a Ka'a State Park

Nahiku

10

Ridge Trail

Kaumahina State Park

Ke'anae Arboretum

Wailua Valley Lookout

Waikani Falls

Waianapanapa

11

Waianapanapa State Park

Pailoa Bay

Waianapanapa Coastal Trail

360

🚻 🔺

✈

🚻 ⛽ 💧

Hana

Hana Bay

Ka'uiki Head

12

'Alau Island

Hamoa Beach

31

aleakala National Park

Pailkea Stream

Waiho'i Stream

Kipahulu Valley

Wailua Falls

Makahiku

Kaupo Gap

'Ohe'o Gulch

Kipahulu 🔺 **13**

⬆
N

Lelekea Bay

Mokulau Peninsula

Kaupo

Beyond Kipahulu

14

Pacific Ocean

Island of Maui (shown)

Pā'ia

A FEW MILES EAST OF KAHULUI THE HĀNA HIGHWAY (RTE. 36) SKIRTS THE AIRPORT AMIDST ACRES OF SUGAR CANE, THEN HEADS ON THROUGH THE PARTIALLY REVIVED OLD PLANTATION TOWN OF *PĀ'IA* (PRON. "PAH-EE-AH,"MEANING "NOISY"), THE LAST COMMERCIAL CENTER BEFORE HĀNA. UNTIL A FEW DECADES AGO, PĀ'IA INCLUDED SEVERAL OUTLYING VILLAGES HOUSING THOUSANDS OF SUGAR PLANTA-TION WORKERS. THIS ERA OVERLAPPED WITH MAUI'S "HIPPIE" PERIOD (1970S ONWARDS), WHICH STILL MINGLES WITH ITS SUBSEQUENT REPUTATION AS ONE OF THE WINDSURFING CAPITALS OF THE WORLD.

PĀI'A'S UNIQUE CLUSTER OF CONTEMPORARY MERCHANTS—MAUI'S "SOUTH SEAS TRADING POST"—ALSO SPECIALIZE IN ISLAND-FABRICATED HANDICRAFTS, ART AND CLOTHING. POTENTIAL PICNICKERS CAN PICK UP FOOD-TO-GO HERE, BEING MINDFUL THAT ROADSIDE FRUIT STANDS *EN ROUTE* OFFER DELICIOUS, MAUI-GROWN TROPICAL FRUITS, GREEN COCONUT WATER, HOT LUNCH DISHES AND OTHER TASTY MUNCHIES.

DON'T FORGET TO FILL YOUR CAR UP WITH GASOLINE; THERE'S NONE AVAILABLE UNTIL YOU REACH HĀNA—52 MILES, 617 CURVES AND 56 BRIDGES LATER.

PĀ'IA IS AN EXCELLENT AREA FROM WHICH TO OBSERVE 10,020-FOOT HALEAKALĀ, THE ENORMOUS DORMANT VOLCANO THAT DOMINATES EAST MAUI, PROVIDING SPECTACULAR TOPOGRAPHY AHEAD.

THE BEST BEACHES ALONG THE ENTIRE HIGHWAY ARE RIGHT HERE: H. A. BALDWIN AND HOOKIPA COUNTY PARKS. THE LATTER IS WORLD-RENOWNED FOR ITS SUPERB WAVES, BEARING OUTSTANDING "REGULAR," WIND- AND KITE-SURFERS. A LOCAL FAVORITE, HO'OKIPA IS NEVERTHELESS DANGEROUS TO SWIMMERS UNAC-CUSTOMED TO HIGH SURF, STRONG CURRENTS AND ROCKY COASTLINES. COVERED PAVILIONS OVERLOOKING THE COAST PROVIDE AN EXCELLENT BREAKFAST SPOT FOR EARLY BIRDS DRIVING TOWARDS HĀNA.

(ABOVE) A window of **sunrise light** highlights ʻĪao Valley (West Maui), viewed from Pāʻia, the beginning of Maui's famous Hāna Highway, one of the most spectacular drives in the entire Pacific.

(LEFT) The staff of life elsewhere in the Pacific, **coconuts** *(Cocos nucifera)* are little-used in Hawaiʻi. Here they are considered a primarily decorative tropical "feather duster" which unfortunately bears nuts that may fall on people's heads, inviting lawsuits! This Tongan palm-trimmer hacks energetically at dead fronds and developing nuts.

(OPPOSITE PAGE) The Kahului-Pā'ia area is dominated by **sugarcane,** a giant grass and one of Maui's major industries. Covering almost 37,000 acres, Maui's sugar totals 200,000 tons each year.

(RIGHT) **Hibiscus** (*Hibiscus rosa-sinensis X schizopetale*) blooms all-year in Pā'ia, as elsewhere on Maui. Each blossom lasts at least one day without water.

(ABOVE) **Pā'ia Mantokuji Mission,** with its shapely oriental architecture, colorful cemetery and authentic Japanese gong, reminds us of the strong Buddhist faith of many Mauians.

(LEFT) In summer, **royal poincianas** *(Delonix regia)* burst forth with masses of flaming crimson-orange flowers amid feathery, apple-green foliage.

(LEFT) **Ho'okipa beach park.** "Regular," wind-, and kite-surfers, flecking the ocean with brilliantly colored "sea butterflies" whizz down waves powered by arctic storms. Inshore wave intensity is broken by an inner sandstone ledge, enabling children to play safely in shallow pools. Fishermen favor rocky cliff ledges.

Photo by Cameron Kepler

(ABOVE) Whether tortuously tossing amidst the fury of a storm, breaking with turquoise and glassy edges or arching back in curving rooster tails, Ho'okipa's waves are ever-changing, ever-beautiful and often awesome. Their shape, color and dynamism add dimension to Maui's natural beauty. Each of four major surfing breaks accommodates surfers of varying levels of competence. Admire the skillful wave riders from viewing areas above the cliffs.

(ABOVE) Particularly familiar to lowlanders, the **cane toad** or giant neotropical toad (locally "bufo" or "poloka") may be encountered sleeping in roadside grass or pitifully squashed on roads after dark. Chunky and squat, with warty, dry skin, cane toads were introduced from Puerto Rico in 1932 in efforts to control a plethora of alien insects plaguing sugarcane fields. Watch for their large tadpoles crowding muddy ponds along the highway or, if you are traveling at night, listen for their deep, throaty croaks penetrating the otherwise quiet air.

Ha'ikū

PINEAPPLES! THEIR PRESENCE INDICATES A CHANGING CLIMATE. MAUI'S SEMI-ARID ISTHMUS ("VALLEY"), SUPPORTING EXPANSES OF IRRIGATED SUGAR, IS NOW LEFT BEHIND. HA'IKŪ (PRON. "HIGH-KU") TOWNSHIP, HIDDEN CLOSE UPSLOPE, RECEIVES OVER 50 INCHES OF RAIN ANNUALLY IN CONTRAST TO PĀ'IA'S 30 INCHES, AND IS COOLER AND MORE HUMID.

THE SEASHORE IS FRONTED BY CLIFFS OF EVER-INCREASING HEIGHT AS THE SEA NIPS INTO HALEAKALĀ. BAYS ABOUND AND CONCEALED WATERFALLS PLUNGE INTO LUSH PRECIPITOUS VALLEYS AND WAVES CRASH MIGHTILY AGAINST ROCKY HEADLANDS.

HERE IS THE LAST EASY SECTION OF TRAVEL UNTIL HĀNA. TWISTING GENTLY, THE REAL HĀNA HIGHWAY BEGINS (RENUMBERED 360) AT THE JUNCTION WITH HWY. 365 (KAUPAKALUA ROAD). SOON THE WRITHING NARROW MOUNTAIN ROAD SLOWS TRAFFIC TO A CRAWL.

NOW IS THE TIME FOR NEW SIGHTS, TASTES, SMELLS AND SOUNDS. THE GRIP OF CIVILIZATION LOOSENS. DON'T WORRY ABOUT RAIN SQUALLS; IT MAY (OR MAY NOT) BE CLEAR AHEAD.

WHILE DRIVING THIS FIRST SECTION, NOTICE GRADUAL TRANSFORMATIONS AS THE ROAD MOVES ONTO HALEAKALĀ'S EVER-STEEPENING FLANK. ALTHOUGH PASTURELANDS THAT HAVE REPLACED PINEAPPLE FIELDS PERSIST, ROADSIDE GRASSES PROGRESSIVELY YIELD TO NATIVE FERNS AND PHILIPPINE GROUND ORCHIDS, WHOSE CLUSTERS OF SMALL MAUVE FLOWERS BEAUTIFY THE ROADCUTS. IN FINE WEATHER, NOTE THE DARK GREEN OF NATIVE FORESTS AT HIGHER ELEVATIONS, WHILE AROUND YOU PATCHY ASSEMBLAGES OF INTRODUCED TREES COMPRISE MAUI'S WINDWARD LOWLAND FORESTS: IRONWOOD, NORFOLK ISLAND AND COOK PINES, CHRISTMAS BERRY, KUKUI, GUAVA, MANGO AND JAVA PLUM (THE LAST THREE ARE EDIBLE).

(RIGHT) All roadside fields are commercial: it is illegal to pick pineapples unless you grow them on your own land. They have been grown on a large scale in Hawai'i since 1886, when the outstanding 'Smooth Cayenne' variety was introduced to the islands.

(ABOVE) A luscious pineapple fruit and composite flower. Botanically classified in the bromeliad family *Bromeliaceae*, pineapples are native to tropical America, where their native habitats are rather dry

(RIGHT) In 2000, the Hāna Highway became a Millennium Legacy Trail, celebrated by a **Millennium monument** on the grassy corner with Hwy 365 (Kaupakalua Rd.) In the future, it is hoped that this magnificent highway will be designated a National Heritage Corridor.

(TOP) **Hanehoi Valley cliffs**. Eastward, beaches are scanty, all composed of gray volcanic sand. Sand color is dominated by the presence of *lava outcroppings* rather than by *coral reefs*, absent on this coast.

(BOTTOM) Seaward lies a rugged coast, replete with steep valleys, lush vegetation, waterfalls, bays, islands and rocky points. Unfortunately these are only accessible to hikers with prior permission from private landowners or East Maui Irrigation Company.

(ABOVE) **Passion fruit:** visions of aphrodisiacs and associated delights spring to mind *vis-a-vis* this delectable tropical fruit. However, when named by Spanish settlers in tropical America, passion fruit reminded them not of worldly pleasures but of the sufferings of Christ. Each portion of the plant symbolized an aspect of the crucifixion: the 10 petals represented Jesus' apostles, the floral "fringe" a crown of thorns, three knobbed styles the Holy Trinity, etc.

(TOP) Shining a brilliant green, the vine's tri-lobed leaves portray the fingered hands of Christ's prosecutors. A common vine, trailing along roadside vegetation, the passionfruit vine is locally called *liliko'i*, after Lilikoi, a land division in Ha'ikū, where the vine first ran wild in Hawai'i.

(BOTTOM) In India, Buddha is sometimes pictured sitting beneath the **rose apple's** *(Syzygium jambos)* full-foliaged branches. Bearing abundant yellow pompom blossoms and pastel greenish-pink "fruits of immortality" all year (primarily August to October), the tree came from India as an ornamental.

(BELOW) The fruit's pinkish flesh is firm, with a delicate rose taste: tender, non-acidic, sweet. Rose apples are best fresh (very ripe or bruised). Since escaping from cultivation, rose apple's dark thickets are characteristic of Maui's newly evolving lowland forests.

(TOP) Little purple clusters of **Philippine ground orchids** *(Spathoglottis plicata)*, peeking through pleated leaves and roadside ferns, brighten roadsides from Ha'ikū to Kīpahulu. You will not see any of Maui's own native orchids: few, tiny, greenish, and extremely rare, they are restricted to drippy rain forests and high elevation bogs.

(MIDDLE) With fronds shaped like breadfruit leaves, the ***laua'e*** (pron. "la-wah-ee"), *Microsorium scolopendria,* is one of Maui's well-known and prettiest ferns. Its snaky green stems (rhizomes) creep and intertwine, mat-like, along the ground, sending up shiny, leathery leaves. Large, indented, circular spore clusters dot the fronds' finger-like lobes on their undersides. In ancient Hawai'i, *laua'e* symbolized romantic love.

(BOTTOM) Native to Brazil but common in Maui's lowlands, **Christmas berry** *(Schinus terebinthifolius)* is most noticeable during the fall, when dense clusters of scarlet berries brighten roadsides. Although ideal for wreaths and holiday decorations, they are inedible.

(TOP & MIDDLE) Hop out of your car and you're bound to step on some tiny puffs of delicate pink in low, prickly mats. Touch a few leaves and they suddenly "play dead" (little bladders at the base of the leaves release stored water that seeps into air spaces). A few minutes later, slowly at first, the entire **sensitive plant** *(Mimosa pudica)* "comes alive" again. What a remarkable adaptation to avoid being eaten by mammals!

(BOTTOM) Another common roadside weed, often associated with sensitive plant, is the thornless, yellow-flowered **partridge pea** *(Chamaecrista nictitans)*. Native to tropical America, it has been in Hawai'i since the mid-19th century. Its scientific name means "low plumes."

Kailua

NEATLY-TRIMMED GARDENS WITH COLORFUL FLOWERS GREET YOU AS YOU DRIVE INTO THIS ATTRACTIVE, VERY MAUIAN OUTPOST OF CIVILIZATION, FIELD HEAD-QUARTERS OF THE EAST MAUI IRRIGATION COMPANY (EMI). A COMPANY TOWN, MOST RESIDENTS WORK ON THE EXTENSIVE DITCH SYSTEM THAT DELIVERS WATER COLLECTED FROM HALEAKALĀ'S NORTH SLOPE TO CENTRAL AND UPCOUNTRY MAUI (THE STATE OF HAWAI'I IS UNUSUAL IN THAT IT ALLOWS PRIVATE COMPANIES TO SHARE CONTROL OF ITS WATER RESOURCES). STOP TO LOOK AT THE DAMS (NOTABLY AT MILE MARKER 8), DIVERSIONS, METAL GRIDS TO KEEP OUT DEBRIS, AND DEEP DARK TUNNELS CHANNELING THROUGH THE MOUNTAIN. ALTHOUGH THE HIGHWAY WAS BASICALLY CONSTRUCTED USING BULLDOZERS, THE DITCHES WERE HAND-HEWN BY IMPORTED ASIAN LABOR.

KAILUA (PRON. "KYE-LOO-AH") IS A QUIET TOWN WITHOUT EVEN A STORE. WHAT A DRAMATIC CHANGE FROM THE EARLY 1900S, WHEN CRIMINALS WERE BANISHED TO KAILUA'S PRISON CAMP, THEN THE END OF THE ROAD, FROM WHENCE ONLY A TRAIL EXTENDED FURTHER EAST!

(ABOVE) **O'opuola Gulch,** one of dozens of ravines along the highway, is heav-ily studded with rounded masses of whitish *kukui (Aleurites moluccana)* foliage. In past eras, residents gathered the *kukui's* prolific oily nuts for medi-cines, ingenious candles and torches. Resembling tough-shelled walnuts, these nuts may cause intestinal distress if eaten. A contemporary use is in threading the polished black seeds into leis.

(ABOVE) Shady **kukui trees** and other roadside vegetation near O'opuola Gulch.

(RIGHT) **Kukui leaves** sparkle in morning sunshine. Although their leaves are maple shaped, the *kukui* is totally unrelated to maples.

(BOTTOM) **Common guava trees** *(Psidium guajava)* grow abundantly along large stretches of highway, flanking roadsides and heavily dotting pastures. Their medium-height bushes bear circular, lemon-sized fruits—sweet, tasty and acidic—that are delicious when fresh.

(RIGHT) Select large, softish guavas with rounded knobby skins and dark-pink flesh. Watch for fruitflies hovering around the rotting, fallen fruit, and, PLEASE, don't even *think of* smuggling guavas back to the mainland! (The California Fruit Growers' Association will suffer gargantuan fruit losses if fruitflies ever start stinging their crops.)

(OPPOSITE PAGE) Over 50 miles of tunnels and 23 miles of ditches, mostly hand-hewn like these at O'opuola Gulch, comprise East Maui Irrigation's (EMI) **ditch system,** a monument to early 20th century Asian labor. If you plan to walk more than a stone's throw from your car (except at public stopping areas), or hunt pigs, previous signed permission is essential from the EMI office in Pā'ia.

(ABOVE) Unfurling yellow in the morning, turning orange in the afternoon and withering by nightfall, *hau* (rhymes with cow), or wild hibiscus, *Hibiscus tiliaceus,* continually buds off heart-shaped leaves and hibiscus blossoms that ancient Polynesians identified with the ephemeral human spirit.

(LEFT) Along certain sections of the highway (e.g., Kailua, Wailua), roadside pruning periodically exposes impenetrable tangles of branches. It's easy to understand why *hau* horrifies backpackers! Extremely useful, *hau* provided abundant commodities for early Polynesian settlers: cork-like fishing floats, medicines, ropes and clothing.

(THIS PAGE & FACING PAGE) **Yellow**, **white** and **kahili gingers** (*Hedychium coronarium, H. flavescens, H. gardnerianum*, respectively), used for decoration and leis, are numerous along the entire highway. Of Asian origin, their clusters of showy, butterfly-shaped flowers are irresistibly aromatic. Even their pink rhizomes (which unfortunately choke out native vegetation) smell tantalizingly sweet. Pick a blossom, nip off the bottom one-eighth inch and suck a few drops of its sweet, gingery nectar from the elongated flower tube. It's delicious.

(LEFT) **Allamanda's** (*Allamanda cathartica*) large, bright yellow, velvety flowers are unmistakable. A good area to spot their sprawling vines (which may climb trees) is just east of Kailua. From tropical Brazil, their orange-sized tubular blossoms expand from a brown throat into five rounded petals.

(BELOW) Dazzling sprays of the **mountain apple's** (*Eugenia malaccensis*) cerise, miniature shaving brushes present a dazzling sight during May and June. This "very Hawaiian" near-native fruit originally came to the islands in Polynesian voyaging canoes from the Marquesas Islands to the south.

(RIGHT) Months after blooming, pink-and-white, waxy, thin-skinned fruitshang from the mountain apple's branches and trunks. Many trees perch on steep gullies, their tempting fruits dangling just beyond reach. Juicy, pear-like and refreshing, they unfortunately do not keep well, even refrigerated.

(ABOVE) Don't be reticent about sampling wild **strawberry guavas** or *waiwi* (pron. "vai-vee"), *Psidium cattleianum*. An inch in diameter, and particularly prevalent in September and October, these tasty, red-purple fruits from Brazil cook into excellent jam as well as providing sweet, juicy snacks.

(LEFT) Strawberry guava's shrubby trees, covered with glossy, elliptical leaves are, in places, replacing Maui's native forests. They are "noxious weeds," so eat away! Note that they are less acidic than common guavas.

Waikamoi

(FACING PAGE) Waikamoi Nature Trail: stretch your legs along this delightfully lush forested trail, complete with rewarding views.

(LEFT) Maui's lowland forests, a lush mix of native and introduced vegetation.

WINDING THROUGH MOIST LOWLAND FORESTS, THE ROAD ALMOST LEAVES BEHIND OPEN COUNTRY. THE WAIKAMOI (MEANING "WATER ACQUIRED BY THE THREADFIN FISH," PRON. "WHY-KA-MOY") REGION INCLUDES BAMBOO FORESTS, EUCALYPTUS, PAPERBARK, GINGERS, HELICONIAS AND TROPICAL VINES. VEGETATION IS WILDER, LUSHER, MORE VARIED AND, TYPICAL OF ALL HAWAI'I'S LOWLANDS, INTRODUCED FROM OTHER PARTS OF THE WORLD: ASIA, AUSTRALIA, SOUTH AMERICA AND POLYNESIA.

MAUI HAS NO TRUE "JUNGLES" IN THE POPULAR SENSE, NOR IS IT A "TROPI-CAL PARADISE", BUT FROM HERE TO KĪPAHULU IS A CLOSE APPROXIMATION TO THESE OVERUSED PHRASES. AS YOU PASS THROUGH THE BAMBOO FOREST, RECALL THE WISE WORDS OF BUDDHA (WHO FREQUENTLY SAT IN BAMBOO GROVES), GENTLY ADVIS-ING US THAT TRUE PARADISE IS "WITHIN."

A HALF-MILE BEYOND MILE MARKER 9 LIES WAIKAMOI RIDGE, WHERE HAWAI'I'S STATE DEPARTMENT OF LAND & NATURAL RESOURCES (DLNR) HAS CON-STRUCTED ONE OF MAUI'S FEW PUBLIC TRAILS. HOP OUT OF YOUR CAR, STRETCH YOUR LEGS AND EXPLORE THIS LOVELY, WELL-KEPT TRAIL, WHICH WINDS UP TO A RIDGE WITH VIEWS. SMELL THE DANK, EARTHY AIR, STROLL THROUGH TALL TREES ADORNED WITH LARGE, HEART-LEAVED TARO VINES, PEER CLOSELY AT HELICONIA AND GINGER FLOWERS AND ADMIRE THE FILTERED LIGHT FALLING ON LACY FERNS.

(LEFT) **Heliconias** are popular ornamentals that lend a distinctive South American flavor to many portions of the Hāna Highway. Brilliant orange-red **common lobster claws** (*Heliconia bihai*) sport huge banana-like leaves. Their common name derives from alternating, claw-shaped "floral boats" colored like boiled lobsters. Within each "boat" (a modified leaf) arise the true flowers—inconspicuous and greenish.

(BELOW) Lucky hikers find **"star fungi"** (here beside a fallen guava). Tropical and subtropical regions the world over are notoriously poor in mushrooms compared to colder regions, so it is always a pleasure to discover such gems.

(RIGHT & BELOW) Waikamoi is famous for its extensive **bamboo forests** (*Bambusa vulgaris*) which dominate the area and date back to the misty realms of Hawaiian mythology. Progenitors of this grove are thought to have been brought to Maui by Pele's sister, Hi'iaka, from Tahiti.

Photo by Cameron Kepler

Photo by Cameron Kepler

(LEFT) Generating an Asian ambience, bamboo's **jade or golden culms** tower skywards. Old-timers collect the long conical shoots (permits are necessary from DLNR) for cooking; however, unless properly cut, soaked and pre-boiled they taste bitter.

(BELOW) The stately bamboos, mantled with elliptical, **feathery foliage**, are particularly appreciated along streams, where they arch towards light. Creative artists utilize bamboo's satin-smooth culms for flutes, elegant ornaments, Japanese-style vases and fishing poles.

(ABOVE) Shady gullies spawn trickling cascades that nurture mosses and ferns, including delicate **maidenhair ferns** *(Adiantum raddianum).*

(BELOW) Squeeze one of the reddish "cones" of **shampoo ginger** *(Zingiber zerumbet)*, the understory, broadleaf flowering plant that lines Waikamoi Ridge Trail for quite a way. Introduced centuries ago into Hawai'i, this knee-high Polynesian wild ginger exudes copious quantities of a perfumy, slippery sap, utilized for a massage lubricant and shampoo centuries before European men arrived.

(ABOVE) Spirally festooning paperbark and eucalyptus trees along Waikamoi Ridge Trail, lending a tropical flavor to the vegetation, South American **taro vines** *(Scindapsus aureus)* are merely runaway houseplants!

Puohokamoa

With waterfalls plunging into swimming-holes, deep abysses flanked by sheer cliffs, and rampant tropical vegetation, Puohokamoa typifies the rugged nature of Haleakalā's north slope. At mile marker 11, where the highway crosses Puohokamoa Stream, a few cars can squeeze into a roadside pullout, but only a few. If the area is crowded, avoid what is sometimes dangerous congestion and keep going, as you will have the opportunity to see other great waterfalls. From the bridge you can view a small, two-channeled waterfall; a short gravel trail leads to a pool at its base. A mini-picnic ground has been developed there, with a covered table in case you get caught by the rain (remember, rain forests are beauti-ful *because* of the rain they receive!).

A brief walk along the path quickly leads you through a sampling of lush vegetation typical of Maui's entire Hāna Highway: *kukui* nut trees, *ti*, heliconias, impatiens, gingers, "red" bananas, etc., all mingled with entwining taro vines.

(facing page) An extremely short, sturdy trail tunnels through a profusion of tropical lushness to a double **waterfall** and swim-ming hole at Puohokamoa Stream.

(left) Yellow gingers and bunchy **ti** (*Cordyline terminalis* or *C. fru-ticosa*) leaves luxuriate wildly beneath maple-leaved *kukui* trees. Prior to the days of alu-minum foil, plastic wrap, aspirin, beer, plates, flags and raincoats, the Polynesian-introduced *ti*, with its big shiny, elliptical leaves, served a variety of house-hold, community and military purposes, viz., peace symbol during war.

(LEFT) Below the road (and invisible from it), Puohokamoa steepens into a precipitous **V-shaped valley** (note car in photo). A ribbon waterfall plunges more than 200 feet into a shallow pool, from which ascent is virtually impossible.

(BELOW) Puohokamoa is at 550-feet elevation, about a half-mile from the sea. Offshore and inaccessible from land lies a picturesque, double-humped sea stack, which you may recognize from the movie *Jurassic Park*. **Keōpuka Rock**, 140-feet high, defies climbing, thus is a haunt only for a few seabirds such as black noddies. Coastal plants, some rare, cling precariously to its near-vertical sides.

(RIGHT) Terrain studded with geologically **young ravines** all along the Hāna Highway allow us to glimpse the numerous (and often insurmountable) topographic difficulties faced by the road's original construction workers. They are impressive demonstrations of the enduring victory of water over rock.

(BELOW) For several miles you have passed roadbanks blanketed with Hawai'i's native **false staghorn fern** (*uluhe, Dicranopteris linearis*). Its hardy fronds, about one-foot across, divide successively in twos, producing tangled mats of applegreen fernery which colonize and protect steep slopes from erosion.

(ABOVE) *Uluhe* looks quite innocuous as you drive along, but try negotiating a ridge of it. Stiff, wiry, entangling stems bind together tight greenery which can rise up to 20-feet high in compact thickets that challenge the staunchest hikers.

(FACING PAGE) Here is the long-sought **Garden of Eden**! Located at mile maker 10.5 (west of Puohokamoa Falls), a stunning subtropical garden, bursting with notable Polynesian plants and a remarkable array of flowering and fruiting trees. All are displayed by an award-winning landscape designer. Easy, well-maintained trails wind circuitously amid labeled plants. In 1995, this garden was applauded by the State of Hawai'i for its conservation/land management techniques. Pictured are **star fruit** (*Averrhoa carambola*, RIGHT) and a rare tropical delicacy, the famous Asian **durian** (*Durio zibethinus*, LEFT).

The Muddy Water Story

VISITORS AND RESIDENTS ALIKE WONDER WHY WATER FLOWING OVER THE HĀNA HIGHWAY'S WATERFALLS IS SO MUDDY, AND WHETHER IT IS SAFE TO DRINK.

RAIN FORESTS ABOVE THE HIGHWAY, EXTENDING ACROSS THE ENTIRE WIND-WARD SLOPE OF HALEAKALĀ, CONTAIN LARGE POPULATIONS OF INTRODUCED FERAL PIGS, WHOSE ROOTING AND "ROTOTILLING" ACTIVITIES, COUPLED WITH STEEP SLOPES AND HEAVY RAINFALL, CAUSE EXTENSIVE DAMAGE TO MAUI'S WATERSHEDS.

NATIVE FORESTS BETWEEN 2,500- AND 7,000-FEET ELEVATION ARE PARTICU-LARLY VULNERABLE. THE RESULTANT EROSION DEGRADES MAUI'S WATER QUALITY, DESTROYS THE PRISTINE FORESTS, INTRODUCES DISEASE, ENDANGERS BIRDS AND PLANTS, PRODUCES THE MUDDY WATER WHICH FLOWS OVER WATERFALLS AND CRE-ATES MURKY SWIMMING IN OTHERWISE DELIGHTFUL SWIMMING HOLES. MAUI'S STREAMS CONTAIN BACTERIAL COUNTS WHICH EXCEED FEDERAL STANDARDS: **DO NOT DRINK STREAM WATER**.

Photo by Cameron Kepler

(ABOVE) Native Hawaiian rain forests: **pristine vegetation**, fast diminishing on Maui and **pig-damaged** vegetation, now more the rule than the exception.

(ABOVE) **Eroded forest debris**, the result of a single storm and previously pig-damaged soil cover, measured 300-feet long, averaging 12-feet wide and 3-feet high on a beach below the Hāna Highway. This impressive mass of leaf litter was washed down by a single stream in the 1980s.

(RIGHT) Cute to play with when *keiki* (young) and exciting to hunt when mature, **wild pigs** were not originally part of Hawai'i's native fauna. They devastate and degrade Maui's watersheds and native forests.

Photo by David Boynton

45

Kaumahina

STOP AT KAUMAHINA (LITERALLY "MOONRISE," PRON. "COW-MAH-HEENAH") FOR A DRAMATIC COASTAL VIEW THAT PROVIDES YOUR FIRST GLIMPSE OF THE PICTURESQUE, DEEPLY-CARVED HONOMANŪ BAY. FURTHER EAST THE RELATIVELY FRESH LAVAS OF KE'ANAE PENINSULA, AND AN ASSORTMENT OF ODD-SHAPED SEA STACKS AND ROCKY POINTS, SKIRTED WITH WHITE FOAM, JUT INTO ROUGH WATERS.

ONLY 1.2 MILES BEYOND PUOHOKAMOA, KAUMAHINA OFFERS TAP DRINKING WATER, FLUSH TOILETS, REFUSE BINS AND SPACIOUS PICNIC FACILITIES. ALTHOUGH IT IS APPROXIMATELY HALF-WAY TO HĀNA, MUCH OF THE BEST SCENERY LIES AHEAD.

AS YOU STRETCH YOUR LEGS, NOTE SOME OF THE BEAUTIFUL TROPICAL PLANTS THAT THRIVE HERE ON MAUI'S WARM, WET NORTH SLOPE: RED, SHELL, AND TORCH GINGERS; SPIDER LILIES AND TALL BANANAS, ALL UNDER A TREE COVER OF PAPERBARKS, EUCALYPTUS AND THE GOLDEN-FLOWERED FORMOSAN KOA. A NATURE TRAIL OFFERS PLEASANT SAUNTERING AMONGST TALL *HALA* TREES, PERCHED ON TEPEE-LIKE STILT ROOTS.

(FACING PAGE) Spectacular **cliffs** at Kaumahina State Wayside Park. At the furthest point, Ke'anae's lava peninsula juts dramatically into the ocean.

(TOP) Resembling a curved, pendant strand of pink-and-white porcelain shells, blossoms of **shell ginger** (Alpinia zerumbet) emerge from tall, closely-packed leaf blades. These artfully arranged floral necklaces should be at eye level.

(BOTTOM) This exquisite ornamental, native to high elevation cloud forests of Southeast Asia, has been cultivated for so long in Hawai'i it even boasts a Hawaiian name, **'awapuhi luheluhe** ("drooping ginger").

(ABOVE) Composed of numerous layers of pink-red waxy frills, the conical or tooth-shaped flowerheads of **torch ginger** *(Etlingera elatior)* bespeak the luxuriant tropics. Again Nature fools us: the petal-like frills, overlapping in pinecone fashion, are not petals at all but fancy leaves! The true flowers (small, red and yellow curled tongues) peek out between frilly, waxy layers.

(LEFT) Torch ginger's remarkable **buds** and blooms hide among leaves twice as tall as you! Native to Mauritius Island (Indian Ocean), the species has been given many beautiful descriptive names, including "Magnificent, pure light." The 19th century Hawaiians called them *'awapuhi ko'oko'o* ("walking stick ginger").

(RIGHT) Brilliant red, pink and white Giant Sumatran lily, locally dubbed **Queen Emma lily** *(Crinum amabile),* flowering year-round, brightens the park entrance. Smell its enticing fragrance, but please leave for others to enjoy.

(BELOW) **Wedelia's** *(Wedelia trilobata)* dandelion-like daisies, originally from South America, flourish anywhere, sending out creeping runners replete with bright green leaves. You've seen this cheery ground cover in gardens, parks, around hotels and banks and now bordering sections of the Hāna Highway.

Honomanū Bay

SNAKING EASTWARD, THE HĀNA HIGHWAY CLINGS TENUOUSLY TO PRECIPITOUS 300-FOOT SEA CLIFFS, THE HIGHEST YOU WILL ENCOUNTER ALONG THE ENTIRE HIGHWAY. SOON THE LARGE AND U-SHAPED HONOMANŪ BAY ("SHARK BAY," PRON. "HOE-NO-MAH-NOO") INDENTS THE VERDANTLY PALISADED COASTLINE BY ONE-THIRD OF A MILE. INLAND, COASTAL AND SEAWARD VIEWS FROM THE NUMEROUS SERPENTINE BENDS IN THE HIGHWAY TURN THIS INTO ONE OF THE MOST SCENIC SPOTS ON MAUI. DRIVE SLOWLY AND CAREFULLY. BASK IN BEAUTY! INCIDENTALLY, IF YOU ARE TEMPTED TO COMPLAIN ABOUT THE CONDITION OF THE ROAD, JUST ASK ANYONE WHAT IT WAS LIKE BEFORE 1984, AND YOU'LL QUICKLY EXTOL ITS PRESENT VIRTUES.

THE FIRST VIEW OF HONOMANŪ'S SPARKLING WATERS, TERMINATING IN A SURF-POUNDED BOULDERY BEACH, IS BREATHTAKING. UNFORTUNATELY IT IS AN AWKWARD PLACE TO STOP YOUR CAR. SO IMMENSE IS THE VALLEY AHEAD (IT IS THE SECOND BIGGEST ON HALEAKALĀ'S NORTH SLOPE; THE LARGEST IS KEʻANAE, JUST BEYOND) THAT IT IS STILL DEEP AND DIFFICULT FOR BACKPACKERS TO CROSS IT AT 7,000FT ELEVATION, ABOVE TIMBERLINE! WITHIN A MILE YOU WILL BE PRACTICALLY AT SEA LEVEL, SINCE THE ROAD DESCENDS ONTO HONOMANŪ STREAM'S BROAD FLAT, ALLUVIATED VALLEY BOTTOM CLOSE TO ITS OUTLET. FROM THE WAVE-WASHED BEACH AND STREAM ESTUARY (COMPLETE WITH A NATURAL CHILDREN'S PADDLING POOL ON THE KAHULUI SIDE) YOU ARE GRAPHICALLY REMINDED THAT THE HĀNA HIGHWAY INDEED SKIRTS THE FLANKS OF A STEEP MOUNTAINSIDE, WITH PLENTY OF AIR AND JAGGED ROCKS BELOW THE OUTER ROAD EDGE. PERHAPS BY NOW YOU ARE WONDERING WHY THE ROAD IS CALLED A "HIGHWAY."

THE VALLEY'S SLOPES LOOM PRECIPITOUSLY UP TO 1,200 FT ON EITHER SIDE, CONTAINING THE OLDEST EXPOSED ROCKS ON HALEAKALĀ. STREAM EROSION HAS GOUGED OUT A CANYON SO RUGGED THAT, EVEN TWO MILES INLAND, WHERE IT SWELLS INTO A MASSIVE AMPHITHEATER, AN INACCESSIBLE WATERFALL, THE GREATEST OF HONOMANŪ'S STEPPING-STONE FALLS, THUNDERS 400 FEET INTO A MIGHTY GULCH. (MOST OF THIS WATER IS TAPPED UPSLOPE FOR COMMERCIAL IRRIGATION, HENCE THE MEAGER FLOW AT HONOMANŪ'S OUTLET.)

SEVERAL VANTAGE POINTS DOT THE SERPENTINE ROAD AS IT ASCENDS AGAIN, HUGGING THE VERDANT MOUNTAINSIDE. THE SEA GLITTERS FAR BELOW ... OR YOU MAY ENCOUNTER BLUE-GRAY WATERS DAPPLED BY RAINDROPS. PARK AND JUMP OUT TO ENJOY SOME OF THE DRAMATIC PERSPECTIVES OF HONOMANŪ AND ITS PRECIPITOUS SEA CLIFFS.

(LEFT) Looking **inland** (*makai*) up the immense Honomanū Valley.

(ABOVE & BELOW) **Eastward views** of spectacular Honomanū Bay. Watch for surfers here, too.

(ABOVE) Winding, twisting, turning, the road gradually loses elevation, constantly greeting you with **new panoramas**. From Honomanū to Keʻanae is the most dramatic portion of the highway.

(LEFT) Vegetation luxuriates, bursting from every rock and crevice, reaching ever upwards for maximum sunlight in this huge **shady ravine**. Especially prominent are pale-foliaged *kukui* trees (old friends by now), fiery red African tulip trees and spirally twisting pandanus (*hala*).

(RIGHT) This showy African ornamental escaped from cultivation. Its flaming flashes provide a welcome addition to the multi-hued greens so characteristic of this lush coast.

(BELOW) Globes of frilly, tulip-shaped flowers, resembling lopsided cups of molten steel, protrude boldly from the **African tulip tree's** *(Spathodea campanulata)* dark green, compound-leaved foliage. Budding off from a central mass of curved brown buds, rings of these odd-shaped, scarlet-orange flowers (unrelated to real tulips) occur year-round.

(ABOVE & LEFT) Honomanū flats abound in **woody climbers** such as this mature taro vine (resembling a split-leaf philodendron), backlighted by morning sun.

(BELOW) Huge giant taros (*Alocasia macrorrhiza*), known locally as **elephant ears** or *'ape* (pronounced "ah-pay," not "ape"!), thrive in moist spots. They are close kin to taro, of *poi* fame.

(RIGHT) If you peer under their shiny, dark, heart-shaped leaves, you may see elegant **cream flowers**, reminiscent of anthuriums or calla lilies. A true "emergency food," this Asian-Polynesian introduction to Hawai'i is not edible. Both leaves and rhizome ("root") will seriously irritate your digestive system and throat membranes if eaten raw or boiled, due to an abundance of calcium oxalate crystals.

(BELOW) **Westward views** of Honomanū Bay from roadside pullouts as you climb yet again to new sights.

Ke'anae

A. KE'ANAE ARBORETUM

If you enjoy tropical verdure, this lush, free botanical garden, maintained by the State of Hawai'i Department of Natural Resources, is beautiful and educational. A stream bed with papaya trees, guavas and *'ape* (huge, taro-like leaves) on one side, and banks of colorful impatiens and ferns on the other, line the easy path that leads to a well-tended profusion of native and introduced plants in a setting reminiscent of ancient times. It exhibits dozens of labeled, ornamental flowering and fruiting trees, palms, shrubs, gingers and heliconias (many are unusual), plus a section devoted to Polynesian-introduced plants: taro, breadfruit, bananas, *ti*, sugarcane and *wauke* (from which bark cloth or *tapa*, was made).

For the more adventurous stroller, a roughish mile-long hike ascends *mauka* (in land) from the rear of the arboretum. Crisscrossing a rivulet, it ascends through a melange of native and planted forests up to a large flat. **This hike does not require permission.**

Ke'anae (pron. "kay-a-nigh") weather is one of extremes. You may encounter muggy sunshine, pouring rain or both within minutes. Always carry a plastic bag to shield your camera in case you become caught in a sudden downpour. One rule in tropical areas exceeding 100 inches of annual rainfall is: never trust the sun to keep shining!

(ABOVE) Right at the apex of a monkeypod-shaded hairpin turn (just past the YMCA Camp Ke'anae, before the turnoff to Ke'anae Peninsula) and the **Ke'anae Arboretum** sign.

(RIGHT) Reminiscent of double rows of brilliantly painted bird's beaks, **hanging lobster claw's** (*Heliconia rostrata*) two-dimensional, pendant flowers will visually mesmerize casual strollers through the arboretum.

(ABOVE) The palm exhibit includes several species of Maui's own rare **native palms** (*loʻulu, Pritchardia* species). Their finely pleated leaves, downy gray beneath, do not shed fibers at their tips, a distinguishing feature from Chinese fan palms, well-known in tropical landscaping.

(ABOVE) A strikingly beautiful tree, the **breadfruit** (*'ulu, Artocarpus altilis*), is unquestionably not only famous (remember *Mutiny on the Bounty?*) but one of the world's truly great trees in terms of beauty, utility and cultural associations. Its foot-long, glossy leaves, deeply indented, resemble huge leathery hands. Note the sticky white sap, used in olden days for caulking canoes. The world's largest collection of *'ulu* lies only a few miles ahead, at Kahanu Gardens in 'Ula'ino (0.1 miles past mile marker 31).

(RIGHT) Breadfruit's pale green, compound fruits, the size of a baby's head, are formed from hundreds of coaslesced individual flowers, much like a pineapple. Breadfruits vary in quality, depending on variety and stage of ripeness. Deep-fried chips or thin slices of near-ripe fruits, sauteed in butter and garlic, are always palate pleasers. When fully ripe and steamed, baked or microwaved, they are sweet, gooey and simply delicious.

(LEFT & BELOW) **Red and pink gingers** (*Alpinia purpurata*), with their upright crimson floral heads, are real dazzlers, especially in sunshine. Blooming all year, this plant is unusual in that instead of liberating seeds, the mature flowerhead sprouts dozens of leafy seedlings right where it bloomed. Eventually gravity drags these fast-growing plantlets downward, so they can root beside their parent. Nearby is a fine grove of torch gingers.

(ABOVE & RIGHT) The Arboretum houses a fine variety of **bananas** (*ma'ia, Musa acuminata*), edible and ornamental. Bananas were originally transported to Hawaii by early Polynesian voyagers, but were never relied upon as staple foods as in the rest of Oceania. In fact (with few exceptions), if a Hawaiian woman was caught eating a banana, she was severely punished, perhaps even killed.

(LEFT) One banana clump, of centuries-old lineage in Hawai'i, is **mai'a hē'ī** (Tahitian *fei*), near the far end. It is a special Pacific species (*Musa fehi*) which produces golden fruit on *upright* stalks!

(BELOW) **Hawaiian sugarcane** (*ko, Saccharum officinarum*), introduced 1,500-years ago by early Polynesian settlers, was the sweetest item in their diet until Captain Cook arrived in 1778. At Ke'anae are displayed several old varieties with redder stalks and less fibrous matter than commercial sugar. Other *ko* collections are at the Maui Botanical Garden (Kahului) and Kahanu Garden ('Ula'ino/Hāna).

(FACING PAGE) **Taro** (*Colocasia esculentum*) was, and still is, of deep spiritual and cultural significance in Hawai'i. From its date of Polynesian introduction (about 400 A.D.), it evolved into nearly 200 different varieties, some of which have been preserved at Ke'anae. Note their imaginative names: a black-stalked green-leaved one is *hāpu'u* (recalling its resemblance to *hāpu'u* tree ferns), a stripey-stalked one is *manini* (eching patterns on its namesake reef fish). The layout of taro patches (*lo'i*), the irrigation system and the bananas growing on upraised earth banks, are all features gleaned from ancient Polynesia.

B. KE`ANAE PENINSULA

ACCORDING TO HAWAIIAN LEGEND, KE'ANAE PENINSULA WAS THE FIRST SPOT ON MAUI TO BE BLESSED WITH WATER. IN THE DAYS WHEN THE GREAT GODS OF CREATION, KĀNE AND KANALOA, FIRST INHABITED THESE ISLANDS, THE LAND WAS PERFECTLY DRY. HOWEVER, ON ONE PARTICULAR VISIT TO KE'ANAE, KĀNE, WITH A MOSES-STYLE FLOURISH OF POWER, THRUST HIS WOODEN STAFF INTO SOLID ROCK AND WATER GUSHED FORTH! SINCE THAT MOMENT KE'ANAE (LITERALLY, "INHERITANCE FROM HEAVEN") AND WATER HAVE BEEN INSEPARABLE COMPANIONS.

GEOLOGICALLY, TOO, KE'ANAE IS OUTSTANDING ... AND OF RECENT ORIGIN. GEOLOGISTS ESTIMATE THAT ONLY 1,500–1,200-YEARS AGO, ITS WATER-WORN VALLEY WAS INUNDATED BY IMMENSE LAVA FLOWS. THIS LAVA, SPEWED OUT FROM HALEAKALĀ'S MASSIVE CALDERA, FUNNELED AND CLUNKED DOWN 9,000-FEET ELEVATION, EVENTUALLY SPILLING INTO THE SEA, CREATING A FRESH PENINSULA THAT EVEN TODAY LOOKS RECENT.

IMAGINE CLOUDS OF HISSING, SUPER-HEATED STEAM RISING INTO THE AIR AS THIS FIERY MOLTEN ROCK, FRESH FROM THE BOWELS OF THE EARTH, TUMBLED UNCONTROLLABLY INTO THE PACIFIC'S COOL WATERS. EN ROUTE, THE ERUPTION WIDENED THE ORIGINAL VALLEY'S CONTOURS, BURYING THEM UNDER HUNDREDS OF FEET OF FRESH LAVA. DO STOP AT THE WAILUA WAYSIDE OVERLOOK (MAIN ROAD, 0.4 MI. EAST OF THE KE'ANAE VILLAGE TURNOFF). THIS POINTS YOUR EYES *MAUKA* (INLAND) TO VIEW THE ENORMOUS, CLIFF-FLANKED, LAVA PATHWAY, KO'OLAU GAP, NOW ALMOST COMPLETELY VEGETATED. THE LOOKOUT TRAIL AND STEPS PASS THROUGH A TANGLED *HAU* (WILD HIBISCUS) THICKET, WELL MAINTAINED FOR YOUR CONVENIENCE ... WATCH THE MOSSY, SOMEWHAT SLIPPERY STEPS.

THERE ARE FEW ACCESSIBLE SPOTS IN THE HAWAIIAN ISLANDS THAT RIVAL THE PHYSICAL BEAUTY AND POLYNESIAN CHARM PROVIDED BY KE'ANAE. (TO LOCALS, IT'S MIGHTY GOOD FISHING HERE, TOO!)

(ABOVE) From 7,900-feet high, Ke'anae's **wave-thrashed shores** trace a white curve. Up at this elevation, a jumbled mass of "topographical inconveniences"—deep gullies, waterfalls, sheer rock faces, slippery streams, blind ridges—average 25 gullies every contour mile, a challenge to even experienced woodsmen (and woodswomen too!).

Photo by Ron Nagata/Haleakalā National Park Service

(ABOVE) A **helicopter view** down Ko'olau Gap, as the now-forested lava tumbles from Haleakalā National Park's erosional depression (formerly "crater") all the way to Ke'anae Peninsula.

(ABOVE) Watching the powerful waves crashing against the crinkly black, jagged rocks, we sense a renewed awareness of Maui's recent volcanic origins (the entire island is only 400,000- to 1.3-million-years old.) The rough, **clinkery lava** is one of Hawai'i's two major lava types, *a'a* (pron. "ah-ah"). The other, *pahoehoe* (pron. "pah-hoyhoy"), smooth-surfaced and ropey, is best seen at Hawai'i National Park on the Big Island, but it is here, too. Notice the few inhabitants of Hawai'i's tide-pools as compared to temperate seashores.

(LEFT) **Pi'ina'au Stream** plunges dizzyingly over cliffs and plunge pools into Ko'olau Gap. Here, annual rainfall exceeds 300 inches, whereas down at the coast it is only 85 inches.

Photo by Cameron Kepler

(ABOVE) **Cultivated taro** *(Colocasia esculenta)* bears large, attractive, arrow-headed leaves, which lend a timeless Polynesian quality to the cultivated farmlands. Comprising the bulk of Ke'anae's flatlands, this agricultural crop provides the bulk of Maui's fresh *poi*. Relished by Hawaiians, *poi* is manufactured from boiled, mashed, fermented taro rhizomes ("roots"). For the non-local, *poi* is tastiest eaten with *laulau* (chunks of beef or pork cooked in a *ti*-leaf wrapping).

(RIGHT) Wetland taro, like rice, requires periodic **water monitoring** for perfect growth. Within its colorful patchwork quilt one can identify various growth stages: fallow ground (brown, no water), fresh baby taro (tiny plants, shallow pond), young taro (pale green, shallow water), and mature plants ready for harvest (dark green, no water visible).

(LEFT) A **coconut grove** adjacent to the taro fields adds protection from salt spray, plus nutrition for residents.

(BELOW) View of **Ke'anae flatlands** from the cut-off road leading shoreward from the highway.

(FACING PAGE - TOP) Serving a close-knit community of extended families, the **Congregational Church** is an historic landmark, having reposed near the peninsula's tip since 1860. Its cool stone walls enclose an unpretentious but very Hawaiian chapel. Outside, graceful coconuts, well maintained lawns and gardens add additional charm. To generate a feeling for the Hawaiians, their names and ways, visit the tiny cemetery.

Photo by Cameron Kepler

68

(ABOVE) **Gardens** are neat and colorful in Keʻanae Village despite the humid climate (encouraging rapid growth) and constant salty winds. Most residents are of Hawaiian descent, living a partly self-sufficient lifestyle. The nearest stores are nearly 30 miles back at Pāʻia or the same distance ahead to Hāna.

(ABOVE) Munch on a memorable picnic in this simple Pacific island setting. Never mind the strong breeze. *Hala* (*Pandanus odoratissimus*) trees, considered a nature spirit in old Hawai'i, provided materials for housing, clothing, food, medicine, ornaments, fishing implements and religious rituals for centuries. Notice the spirally tufted leaves and root-stilts, adaptations for their inclement environment.

(TOP) A **parrot's beak heliconia** (*Heliconia psittacorum*) with its orange "parrot-like" floral parts, is a favorite here. Originally from Central America, dozens of species of heliconias grow exceedingly well on Maui. The parrot's beak is one of the shortest, hardiest, and quick-spreading species.

(MIDDLE) When *hala*'s leaves are de-spined and dried they are woven into durable, glossy **hala mats.** This traditional Polynesian art is still alive in Hawai'i. Nowadays one can buy *hala* mats in Kahului, manufactured laboriously in the Philippines and Tuvalu. *Hala*'s orange "keys," part of a pineapple-like fruit, are edible and, when dry and paintbrush-like, adapted to long-distance ocean dissemination.

(BELOW) A splendid **westward view** from Ke'anae, showing successive points, bays, and offshore rocks.

(TOP & MIDDLE) A haven for seabirds, **Moku mana Islet** looms straight and high, defying human interference. Part of Maui's off-shore refuge system, Moku mana offers protected status to beautiful and uncommon tropical seabirds: great frigatebird, white-tailed tropicbird, and Hawaiian noddy terns. Access to a view is difficult because of private land-holdings.

(BELOW) Steady tradewinds from the northeast, bringing 80–100 inches of rain annually, together with powerful surf, have eroded Ke'anae's coastline into fantastic shapes. Moku mana (literally "life spirit of the birds") and Manahoa ("Needle") Rock are framed within a natural **sea arch** at Pauwalu Point, just east of Ke'anae.

Photo by Cameron Kepler

(ABOVE) Beautiful storm surf, of common occurrence, on a memorable late afternoon at Ke'anae Peninsula.

Wailua to Pua'aka'a

IF YOU ENJOY WATERFALLS, SLOW DOWN HERE. TWISTING AND TURNING, THE ROAD CLIMBS UP TO 1,275 FEET, CROSSING MORE GULLIES. WATER STREAMS IN EVERY CONCEIVABLE MANNER ABOVE AND BELOW THE NEXT FEW MILES OF HIGHWAY, INCLUDING TERRACING CASCADES, "BRIDAL VEILS," LONG SKINNY FALLS OR JUST "PLAIN" ONES. EACH TIME YOU ENCOUNTER THEM THEY ARE DIFFERENT! NATURE PROVIDES OPTIMUM VIEWING CONDITIONS WHEN THE SUN SHINES AFTER HEAVY RAIN, ALTHOUGH AT ANY TIME THEY ARE STUNNING. REMEMBER—THE MORE RAIN, THE MORE WATER AND THE MORE EXQUISITE THE FALLS.

WHEN RAINS BEGIN TO ERODE FRESH TERRAIN, THE FIRST CHANGES TO APPEAR ARE RILLS, FISSURES AND CLEFTS CREATED BY SWIFT-FLOWING STREAMS. AS TIME PROGRESSES, THESE CHANNELS ENLARGE INTO GULCHES, CHASMS, RAVINES, GULLIES, VALLEYS, GORGES AND EVENTUALLY CANYONS. AS HALEAKALĀ CONTINUES ITS EVER-CHANGING LAND SCULPTURING—WHICH RESULTS IN MYRIAD VALLEYS, RIDGES, WATERFALLS AND SEACLIFFS—WE, AS VISITORS OR RESIDENTS TO THIS LOVELY ISLAND, ARE PRIVILEGED TO WITNESS ITS EVOLUTION. IN A MERE 15 MILLION YEARS MAUI WILL HAVE DISAPPEARED FOREVER UNDER THIS AQUEOUS ONSLAUGHT!

(ABOVE) A scenic waterfall, **Kopiliula Stream**, adjacent to the highway.

(ABOVE) So many **waterfalls**—all the way up several thousands of feet. Hawai'i has so many waterfalls that most—such as this one on East Wailua 'Iki Stream at 1,660 feet—are unnamed.

(RIGHT) A nine-year-old Mauian is excited on her first discovery of **Waiokuna Falls.**

(OPPOSITE PAGE & THIS PAGE) There have always been ample rains in this area. **Waterfalls**, gushing after heavy mountain rains, are always a thrill to experience. Ancient Hawaiians, sensitive to even minute changes in weather, composed many chants related to wind and rain:

'Twas in Ko'olau* I met with the rain;
It comes with the lifting and tossing of dust,
Advancing in columns, dashing along,
The rain, it sighs in the forest ...
It smites, it smites now the land ...
Full run the streams, a rushing flood;
The mountain walls leap with the rain.

*Specifically the large valley above the Ke'anae Peninsula; generally, the rain forest encompassing most of Haleakalā's northern slopes.

(LEFT) **Waikani Falls**, fed by pure spring water, on two different days. Note the wedding party's traditional *maile* leis. The long, ribbon falls are fed by the same stream below the highway.

(ABOVE) **Sea stacks** dot the rugged coastline. This cave is accessible only by canoe through a "dragon's teeth" barricade of jagged rocks and tricky winds and swirling currents.

(ABOVE) **Our Lady of Fatima Shrine,** built in 1860, lends a quaint charm to the tiny village of Wailua. The total population of Wailua and its sister village, Ke'anae, is about 150.

(LEFT) Wailua (pron. "Why-loo-ah") boasts impeccably tended gardens, radiating color. **Bougainvillea** (*Bougainvillea glabra*), a nasty-spined, woody vine that beautifies all warm climates, originated in Brazil. It needs full sun, warm temperatures, and heavy pruning to maintain its brilliance, which comes in shades of magenta, purple, yellow, orange, pink and white. Note the *true* flowers (small and white), nestling among collars of colorful bracts (modified leaves). As in heliconias, the bright color first attracting one's eye comes from unconventional *leaves* rather than from *flowers*.

(ABOVE) At mile marker 18.9 is stunning **Wailua Lookout**, well worth a stop. Climb the steps—arched with *hau* tangles—to obtain the best views *mauka* (all the way to the mountaintop) and *makai* (taro patches, coast and village).

(ABOVE) Blechnum ferns (*Blechnum appendiculatum*), common along streams, on road-cuts, beside waterfalls and in all moist places, have no Hawaiian name. Originally from the American tropics, this lovely, small fern is completely "at home" in Hawai'i.

Pua'aka'a to Nāhiku

PUA'AKA'A STATE PARK (PRON. "POO-AH-AH-KAH-AH") IS A DELIGHTFUL STOPPING SPOT. ITS NAME MEANS "PARK OF THE ROLLING PIGS." HELICONIAS, GINGERS, TREE FERNS, GUAVAS AND NATIVE TREES ALL VIE FOR SPACE IN THE RANGY LUSHNESS OF THIS SMALL GARDEN-CUM-PARK. COMPLETE WITH A TRICKLING STREAM MEANDERING THROUGH ITS LAWNS, PICNIC TABLES, POOLS AND WATERFALLS ON TWO LEVELS, IT IS A FAVORITE STOPPING PLACE. CHILDREN CAN WATCH TADPOLES AND BABY FROGS WRITHING ABOUT IN THE SHALLOW POOLS, TOO.

THIS STRETCH OF HIGHWAY, MOVING IN PART THROUGH NATIVE FORESTS, HOVERS AROUND 1,200 FEET, THE HIGHEST ELEVATION WE ENCOUNTER ON OUR TRIP. HERE EMI DITCHES ARE OBVIOUS. ONE PARALLELS THE ROAD, PROVIDING A GLIMPSE OF THE IMMENSE QUANTITIES OF WATER THAT ARE SHUNTED FROM MOUNTAIN TO LOWLAND FOR PINEAPPLE AND SUGAR IRRIGATION.

IF YOU'VE BEEN COUNTING BRIDGES SINCE HA'IKŪ, YOU'RE ADDING QUITE A FEW NOW. SOME GULCHES ARE SO NARROW BRIDGING HARDLY SEEMS NECESSARY, BUT LOOK HOW DEEP AND OMINOUS THE CLEFTS BELOW ARE! PLEASE CONTINUE TO BE A CONSIDERATE DRIVER.

(LEFT) **Picnic area** at Pua'aka'a State Park.

(FACING PAGE - TOP) Three hillocks *(pu'u)* between 1,800 and 3,200 feet scallop Nāhiku's horizon on an exceptionally clear day. Ubiquitous **sword ferns** (*Nephrolepis exaltata*) grow thick and tall in the foreground.

(RIGHT) Do you wonder what lies **upslope?** Waterfalls, pigs, treacherous gullies. Rain guage readings from this area average 390 inches annually, at times exceeding 500 inches. No wonder Nāhiku ranks as the second wettest area in Hawai'i and one of the soggiest in the world!

(LEFT) Hanawī's heavily wooded drainage system hides scenic gems worthy of national park status. From its source at **high elevations** it travels, gently or wildly, through precipitous, bouldery gullies, clothed in fairylands of ferns and mosses.

(LEFT) **Endemic lobelias**, interweaving naturally with endemic trees and shrubs (i.e., only found in Hawai'i) in upper Hanawī, create a time-immemorial native Hawaiian forest that is totally different from the lowlands, which are primarily comprised of introduced vegetation.

(BELOW) **'Ōhā wai** (*Clermontia kakeana*), a lovely native lobelia, can be found not only upslope, but scattered right along in this section of highway. Look for them hanging onto rock faces on the upslope side of the road.

(ABOVE) **Pink clouds** gather over Haleakalā's slopes above Pua'aka'a State Park close to Haleakalā's rim.

(RIGHT) **Hanawī Stream** (photo beside the highway) was the focus of a controversial conservation issue in 1980. The last of East Maui's streams untapped for irrigation, it is a solace for native and endangered species of fish ('o'opu) and a shrimp ('ōpae) that, like salmon, need to travel to the ocean and back to complete their breeding cycle.

Photo by Dann Espy

(LEFT) Below the highway, Hanawī is augmented by cold underground springs beyond the reach of irrigation ditches. In a mighty outburst of energy it thunders over a **200-foot precipice** before emptying into the ocean at Nāhiku.

(BELOW) The **small Indian mongoose** (*Herpestes auropunctatus*) is an introduced, brown, weasel-like pest which has exterminated all Hawai'i's ground-nesting birds. It is present on all islands except Kaua'i. Jokers dub it a "squeasel": a cross between a squirrel and a weasel! Trash cans at Pua'aka'a are a favored hangout.

(RIGHT) **Feral cats** will plead for picnic handouts. Please do NOT feed them! They are rapacious hunters, non-native and devastating to Hawai'i's natural ecosystems.

(BELOW) *'Ōhi'a* (*Metrosideros polymorpha*) is Hawai'i's predominant native tree. Its twisted gray trunks, small rounded leaves and gay red pompons dominate Maui's craggy mountains and valleys, producing a uniquely Hawaiian forest. At Pua'aka'a we skirt the lower edge of the *'ōhi'a* forest, part of the enormous Ko'olau Forest Reserve. Regrettably, few of Hawai'i's forests are pristine, due to feral pig damage, introduced alien plants and a little-understood phenomenon termed "*'ōhi'a* dieback."

Photo by Cameron Kepler

(ABOVE) The curved leaves and widespreading branches of Hawai'i's famous native **koa** (*Acacia koa*) tree occur commonly near Pua'aka'a. *Koa* is confused with Australian eucalyptus, which also possesses curved leaves. *Koa* forests, though diminishing rapidly, are still felled to make furniture, ukuleles, picture frames, and prized bowls. Its reddish, mahogany-like wood flows with beautiful, variegated grains.

(LEFT) In Nāhiku, you'll see attractive plants with lobed leaves and red petioles (leaf stems), the **Ceará rubber tree** (*Manihot glazovii*), closely related to tapioca/manioc (*M. esculenta*), a staple starch in many Pacific islands. Around 1898 entrepeneurs, hoping to "make a million" in an ever-expanding world rubber market, planted about 26,000 trees here. Producing copious amounts of excellent quality rubber, the Nāhiku Rubber Company became outpriced by equally successful plantations elsewhere. It fizzled after ten years.

(ABOVE) **Yellow latispatha** (*Heliconia latispatha*) is very evident at Pua'aka'a. This 3-dimentional heliconia grows rampantly in warm, humid climates and is officially naturalized in Hawai'i. In its native tropical America, it would be pollinated by hummingbirds, whose beaks fit perfectly into the small, curved, greenish flowers arising from the yellow, boat-like bracts.

Wai'ānapanapa

WAI'ĀNAPANAPA (PRON. "WHY-AH-NAH-PA-NAH-PA") STATE PARK IS YET ANOTHER INTERESTING STOP EN ROUTE TO HĀNA, PROVIDING PICNICKING, CAMPING (PERMITS CAN NOW BE ACQUIRED ON-SITE) AND HIKING FACILITIES. ITS RUGGEDLY SCENIC CLIFFS OF CRINKLY BLACK LAVA FLANKED BY THICK NATIVE COASTAL FOREST OFFER A UNIQUE EXPERIENCE FOR THOSE WHO HAVE EXTRA HOURS. THIS IS NOT A PLACE TO RUSH IN AND OUT IN TEN MINUTES.

HERE 120 ACRES HAVE BEEN PRESERVED BY THE STATE OF HAWAI'I, NOT ONLY FOR THEIR NATURAL BEAUTY BUT FOR THE NUMEROUS ARCHAEOLOGICAL SITES: WALLS, HOUSE FOUNDATIONS, *HEIAU* (TEMPLES) AND GRAVESITES. LOOSE-STONED WALLS ABOUND HERE, MARKING LOCATIONS OF DOMESTIC AND RELIGIOUS SIGNIFICANCE. BENEATH RAISED PLATFORMS TOPPED WITH SMOOTH BOULDERS LIE HUMAN BONES THAT ARE STILL RESPECTED BY TODAY'S HAWAIIANS. THEY ARE NOT PLAY AREAS FOR CHILDREN!

ELEMENTAL WATER MUSIC IS STRONG HERE. THE POUNDING THUMPS OF TUMULTUOUS SWELLS BATTERING AGAINST PERFORATED CLIFF FACES PROVIDE A *BASSO CONTINUO* FOR THE INTERMITTENT SWISHES OF FOAM LURCHING UP PA'ILOA'S BLACK SAND BEACH, THE WHOOSHING WATERS CHANNELING WITHIN ROCKY INTERSTICES AND THE EJACULATORY HISSES OF BLOWHOLES.

SUPERIMPOSED UPON THESE MARINE UTTERANCES ARE WILD CRIES OF COMMON AND BLACK NODDY TERNS, RATTLING *HALA* LEAVES, POURING RAIN (USUALLY SHORT, HEAVY SHOWERS) AND PERHAPS WITHIN WAI'ĀNAPANAPA'S EARLY-MORNING STILLNESS THE GENTLE PURRING OF YOUR OWN HEARTBEAT.

(OPPOSITE PAGE) **Crashing surf** on lava at Wai'ānapanapa. Lava flows in this region are, like Ke'anae, geologically very young: only 966–600 years old! Surging waves crash constantly against the jagged rocks, furthering erosion. Their booming is particularly dramatic during storms.

(ABOVE) **Late afternoon** along this uniquely Mauian shoreline recalls Wai'ānapanapa's true meaning, "glistening water." A labyrinth of eroded lava tubes, natural arches and irregular islets lie along this picturesque coast.

(RIGHT) **Jagged rocks** and islands enhance the edge of Wai'ānapanapa's picnic and camping areas. Waves were 23-feet high in Pa'iloa Bay during the 1946 tsunami.

(ABOVE) If you swim at the wave-worn, black pebbly beach at Pa'iloa Bay, watch for small, blue **Portuguese man-o-war** "blad-ders" (*Physalia*) that congregate here. Sometimes the water is so dense with them that, after even a quick dip, your skin will prickle for hours. These little colonial floaters are rarely a problem else-where in the islands. Reef fish occur here, but no coral. Snorkeling should only be tackled by experienced swimmers.

(LEFT) Forests of *hala*, bordered with the bright green native suc-culent **beach naupaka** (*Scaevola taccada*), enhance the rugged beauty of this Pacific-looking area. *Naupaka's* pithy, white seeds, dubbed "hailstones" in the Hawaiian language, possess remarkable tolerance to salt. They can germinate even after one year of immersion in salt water!

(LEFT) **Freshwater caves** are reached by a short, slippery, loop trail from the parking lot. Damp, mossy and luxuriant, the two caves—actually part of a collapsed lava tube—contain two pools, sometimes colored red from thousands of tiny native shrimp that squirm in their shallows. The first pool is a reminder of the princess' blood; the second is the site of a ancient bloody fight between a chief and his unfaithful wife; details are on a wooden sign at the trail entrance.

(BELOW) An easy, three-mile **coastal trail**, part of an ancient *alaloa* ("long trail") that originally extended around the cliff edge, ending in Hāna. Remain on the trail to avoid grazing your toes or twisting your ankles. Tennis shoes or boots are best. Beneath your feet runs a honeycomb of erratic tunnels and gaping pits caused by gases becoming trapped under cooling lava. Watch for the blowhole and *heiau*.

Photo by Cameron Kepler

Photo by Cameron Kepler

(LEFT) **Stone offerings** are sacred. Please respect them. It is inappropriate for non-Polynesians to build *ahu* (rock piles) or wrap *ti* leaves around rocks.

(BELOW) Walking westwards from the park is another cliffside trail (one mile long) to Hāna airport, along which lie ancient **raised gravesites.**

(ABOVE & RIGHT) The delectable perfume of **plumerias** (Common plumeria, *Plumeria rubra*, and Singapore plumeria, *Plumeria obtusa*) bespeak the "romantic tropics." Plumeria trees are dotted around the park for all to enjoy. Pluck one if you wish. Remember, in Hawai'i the right ear means "taken," the left, "available." Smell them at dawn, dusk or during midday heat; they will never disappoint you.

(BOTTOM RIGHT) Down the bumpy, muddy 'Ula'ino (at mile marker 31) road lies Maui's largest ancient temple site, **Hale o Pi'ilani** *heiau*, about 500 years-old, a National Historic Landmark, and possibly the largest remaining ancient structure in Hawai'i. Built entirely from surrounding lava rocks, this massive structure has dimensions which also rival the grandest sites in Polynesia.

(LEFT) The National Tropical Botanical Garden's spacious Kahanu Garden exudes a special ancient Hawaiian spirit. Here, the world's largest collection of **breadfruit** (*'ulu*) varieties (about 150) exemplifies efforts to encourage more people to grow and enjoy this versatile, tasty fruit-cum-vegetable. The Canoe Garden, accompanied by an excellent brochure, is landscaped with "Polynesian-introduced plants" which survived many a mile of salty sea to reach Hawai'i's shores. Pictured is a tasty, soft-spiny species relished by local Filipinos, *pakak* or *kamansi* (*Artocarpus camansi*).

(BELOW) Coastal view from **Kahanu Garden** ("the breath"), open to the public, through spirals of *hala* leaves.

(TOP) The 'Ula'ino ("stormy red") **shoreline** and upper Nāhiku wilderness from offshore. Sea cliffs are absent because the lavas are at least 100,000-years younger than in the area through which you have passed. Up till now, you have encountered lavas of the Kula Series, more than 200,000-years old. From Nāhiku eastwards to Kīpahulu, we travel through lavas of the Hāna Series, less than 100,000-years old.

(RIGHT) Accessible only by canoe, sea arches, basaltic columns and **caves** fascinate adventurous explorers.

(BELOW) **Milky-watered swells** surge into a multi-entranced cave system.

Hāna

Hāna—a special place. It's the most isolated, most tropical, most laid-back, most muggy, most friendly, most "real Hawaiian" community on Maui.

In the early morning you can watch the sunrise develop in both directions as the mountain clouds catch the dawn hues from the eastern sun. Rain pelts you when you barely notice a cloud in the sky. Whales spout offshore and long ribbons of water plunge down precipitous valley walls. Lone fishermen on rocky points throw circular fishnets into choppy blue water. You can pull sizable weeds that you swear were not in your garden two days ago and pick plumerias all year.

Hāna (pron. "Hah-nah") is a place to imbibe Nature's bounteous gifts and glimpse snatches of past Polynesian civilization. Its congenial, take-your-time ambience is very relaxing.

What, you ask, do people do here? They fish, hunt pigs in the forested valleys, grow flowers, rare children, help one another. They work in the hospital, hotels, stores, schools, on roads or for the National Park Service. During off-hours they love to eat, sing, dance, have fun, drink beer, string leis and "talk story" (pidgin for gab).

Hāna's horizons are circumscribed. Activities revolve around the weather and what people feel like doing. You don't have to apologize if you show up late ... or not at all. Life flows pretty smoothly just as it has for centuries. But if a valid controversial issue arises "on the other side" (i.e., anywhere else on Maui) that may affect Hāna residents, many folks jump up and become involved. Their lifestyle is sacred.

Hāna residents are incredibly diverse. You have the locals, mostly of Hawaiian extraction, whose "roots" extend back generations; and the *haoles*, including television personalities and other influential people. The residuum includes leftovers from the 1960s "hippie" era. They range from living in luxury to eking out a simple existence from little plots of land.

However, Hāna does an admirable job of pleasing everyone. Take music. Hāna people love it.

Hāna residents take pride in their gardens, whose upkeep often occupies a good percentage of their recreational time. Don't be fooled by their neatness ... gardening in wet, tropical areas requires constant weeding, extensive trimming, heavy pruning and lugging weekly pickup truckloads of "green waste" to the dump. A dear mainland friend once exclaimed to me: "O, how wonderful, weeds don't even grow in Paradise!"

Kindness, friendliness and cooperation are alive and well in this gentle rural outpost. Residents, of whatever background, share three attributes: happiness, a "plenty-of-time" attitude and ALOHA. But ALOHA may become old with nearly one million people driving by each year. So let your pace be unhurried, your smile genuine and your behavior polite, so that Hāna can remain that "extra special place" for others and for you when you return.

(LEFT) Delightfully lush landscaping at the **Hotel Hāna Maui**. Take a moment to visit their art gallery, featuring a phenomenal variety of art forms by Maui artists: sculpture, painting, wood carving, photography and weaving.

(ABOVE) Resembling a long-necked bird with crest, each **bird-of-paradise** (*Strelitzia reginae*) blends classic poise and floral self-assurance. What perfection of line ... what exoticism! Arising from a boat-shaped, basal sheath, up to six dazzling flowers emerge over a week or two in a sunburst of glossy orange and blue. Year-round beauties, they not only occur fresh but in many artistic guises: quilts, stained glass, paintings, bags, silk clothing and even wind-surfing logos.

(MIDDLE & LEFT) Stunning *obake* **anthuriums** (*Anthurium andraeanum*) thrive in Hāna's high rainfall, warmth and humidity. Symbols of tropical elegance, they originated in Columbia, South America. Denizens of muggy rain forests, they are at home perching on branches amidst the dense shade of multilayered tiers of lush vegetation. They thrive under tree-ferns.

(TOP & MIDDLE) After a predominance of greenery encountered along the highway thus far, Hāna abounds with color. Its gentle muggy breezes waft garden smells everywhere. Gardens and nurserjies such as Hana Tropials and Helani Farm are well worth a visit. Pictured are the ferny-foliaged **pink-and-white** (*Cassia javanica*) and **rainbow shower trees** (*C. X nealae*).

(BOTTOM LEFT & RIGHT) "Tropicals" (heliconias, gingers, tropical foliage) provide a booming cut-flower business in Hāna and Nāhiku. Growers can barely keep pace with the local, national and international demand for these stunning flowers and leaves. Pictured is **Indonesian wax ginger** *(Tapeinochilus ananassae).*

(OPPOSITE PAGE & THIS PAGE) **Heliconias** abound, their foliage resembling bananas, but without trunks. All species require constant warmth, humidity and rain. You have already seen several species *en route* to Hāna. Now you see many more (LEFT TO RIGHT): **Sexy Pink** (*Heliconia chartacea*), **giant lobster claw** (*H. bihai* cv. 'Giant lobster claw'), **Jacquinii lobster claw** (*H. bihai* cv. 'Jacquinii'), and a single bract and flower of **red collinsiana** (*H. collinsiana*) illustrate the startling splendor of these dazzling tropical American imports.

(LEFT) One of Hāna's reliable rains is the *āpuakea*. Following sunrise's heels, it sweeps inland from the ocean, drenching everything and everybody in its inexorable path. Skies turn a clean whitish-gray and Hāna bathes in a clear **yellow dawn light**, reminiscent of the Arctic. These pasture coconuts were photographed around 6 A.M. between several bouts of pouring rain and blinks of sun. Keenly attuned to slight weather changes, ancient Hawaiians named hundreds of localized breezes, winds and rains: "short, sharp winds," "dust-driven winds," "windmist clouds," "pelting rains," etc.

(ABOVE) No trip to Hāna is complete without stopping at the famous **Hasegawa Store**. A legend (even immortalized in song), this *aloha*-filled, delightfully overflowing country store, dating back to 1910, carries everything you need plus more. Film, 2 x 4s, beer or diapers ... Hasegawa's is your place.

(ABOVE AND RIGHT) '**Ālau Island**, 0.3-miles offshore from Hāmoa Beach Road, looms from the far side of a treacherous, rocky channel. Notice the extensive area of white water around it, a warning signal that rip currents and exposed rocks make swimming unsafe in the entire vicinity. Its 150-foot summit, crowned by two, wind-lashed coconut palms, frequently receives generous hatfuls of salty splash.

(LEFT) Tucked within semicircular Mokae Cove lies **Hāmoa Beach**, a restful spot maintained by the Hotel Hāna Maui, with public access and shower. It's a good place to jump in the surf, swim, or just lie in the sun (or rain).

(BELOW) Hāna is a very social place. A rural community, its regular meetings and numerous activities involve large groups. Most weekends provide excuses for a celebration: baby's first birthday, anniversaries, weddings, etc. Hāna residents love to get together and have fun catching pigs, fish and crabs, netting shrimps, and pounding *poi* … then eating them. Churches are important focal points of social life. The **Congregational Wānanalua Church** (center of town), built in 1838, boasts immaculate landscaping and a spacious, acoustically excellent, wooden interior.

(TOP) A few residential streets comprising the small town of Hāna (population 1,200 from Ke'anae to Kaupō) group around **Hāna Bay**. A nice overview of green pastures and distant town can be obtained by walking up to the stone cross (a memorial to Paul Fagan, notable for opening Hāna to tourism).

(BELOW) A **wee girl**, Angel Kalei Maca, who calls Hāna home. Families like hers have plenty to do, but also take time to bask in quietness, simplicity, fresh air and the uncluttered lifestyle at this far eastern end of Maui.

(ABOVE RIGHT) **Papayas** (*Carica papaya*), native to South America, whose seeds came to Hawai'i in the early 1800s. Today these delectable fruits, along with plumerias, Vanda orchids, surfers and hula skirts, practically epitomize island life to the outsider. To be truly sweet, papayas need to be tree-ripened near sea level, bathed in sunshine and rain. Hāna-Kīpahulu orchards provide fruit for markets "on the other side." Papaya plants come in three "sexes": male, female and hermaphrodite (both).

Kīpahulu

KĪPAHULU (PRON. "KEY-PAH-hoo-LOO"): ITS DRIPPING LUSHNESS, BEAUTY, ISOLA-
TION AND GRANDEUR ARE PERSONAL EXPERIENCES. FEEL ITS SALTY AIR; BECOME
DRENCHED, LAUGHINGLY, IN ITS TORRENTIAL RAINS; TASTE ITS SCRUMPTIOUS
PAPAYAS; WONDER AT ITS WATERFALLS; SMELL ITS PERFUMY, DANK AIR; RELISH ITS
RIOT OF COLOR IN RAMBLY GARDENS AND JUNGLY VERDURE; AND MARVEL AT ITS
UNCONQUERABLE PRECIPICES. HUMANS HERE ARE MERE OBSERVERS OF THE POWER-
FUL ELEMENTAL FORCES THAT HAVE SHAPED, AND WILL CONTINUE TO SHAPE, MAUI
FOR MILLENNIA.

WHEN YOU ARRIVE IN KĪPAHULU, YOU MAY FEEL AS IF YOU'VE TRULY STEPPED
BACK INTO HISTORIC HAWAI'I. NATIVE HAWAIIANS HAVE CONTINUOUSLY LIVED AND
WORKED IN THIS AREA FOR CENTURIES. LAYERS OF HUMAN OCCUPATION ARE EVI-
DENT IN THE LANDSCAPE: PRE-CONTACT (PRIOR TO 1778) HAWAIIAN STRUCTURES,
HISTORIC WALLS, RUINS OF SUGAR CANE FLUMES (1890–1925).

THE KĪPAHULU SECTION BECAME PART OF HALEKALĀ NATIONAL PARK WITH
SEVERAL LAND ADDITIONS BEGINNING IN 1951. OF THE 1.4 MILLION PEOPLE WHO
VISIT THE PARK EACH YEAR, 700,000 VISIT THE KĪPAHULU SECTION. THE FIRST PLACE
TO STOP IS THE KĪPAHULU VISITOR CENTER WHICH PROVIDES NATURAL HISTORY AND
CULTURAL EXHIBITS. STAFF MEMBERS OF THE VISITOR CENTER PROVIDE ORIENTATIONS
AND SHORT HIKES AS TIME PERMITS. FOR FURTHER INFORMATION, CALL 248-7375.

(LEFT) **Makahiku Falls** plunges 185 feet into
one of 'Ohe'o Gulch's many turbulent
pools. STAY BEHIND THE RAIL: the precipitous, vertical cliff is undercut. Near here an
overzealous lady once ended up dangling
precariously on the cliff face 30- feet below
its rim, requiring a helicopter with sus-
pended rangers to pluck her off. Such risky
maneuvers are hazardous for both parties.

(OPPOSITE) A very rewarding half-mile hike
passes the splendid Makahiku Falls.
Another 1- ¹/₂ miles traverse a splendid
bamboo forest, ending at spectacular
Waimoku Falls.

THE NATIONAL PARK SERVICE AND RESIDENTS OF THE AREA HAVE BUILT A TRADITIONAL HAWAIIAN HALE (THATCHED HOME) FOR VISITOR VIEWING. VISITORS TO KĪPAHULU CAN ALSO TAKE A HIKING TOUR THROUGH TARO PATCHES WITH A NATIVE HAWAIIAN GUIDE ON THE FIRST TUESDAY OF EVERY MONTH. THE KAPAHU LIVING FARM HAS RESTORED ACRES OF TRADITIONAL TARO PATCHES TO ACTIVE PRODUCTION ALONG WITH OTHER POLYNESIAN FOOD PLANTS.

WHEN HIKING IN THE KĪPAHULU AREA, FREQUENT RAIN CREATES SLIPPERY CONDITIONS AND THE TRAILS ARE OFTEN ROCKY AND UNSTABLE ALONG STREAM BEDS. THE RAIN ALSO ENCOURAGES MOSQUITOS AND FLASH FLOODS, SO BE PREPARED AND WARY.

THE FOLLOWING FOUR TRAILS WHICH PROVIDE ACCESS TO OUTSTANDING SCENERY INCLUDING STREAMS, VEGETATION AND HISTORIC AND CULTURAL SITES, BEGIN AT THE VISITOR CENTER.

KULOA POINT TRAIL IS AN EASY HALF-MILE LOOP TRAIL THAT LEADS DOWN TO THE OCEAN AT KULOA POINT. ENJOY HISTORIC HAWAIIAN ROCK WALLS AND PRE-CONTACT HOUSE SITES AS YOU PASS A HALA (PANDANUS) GROVE AND SEVERAL LARGE POOLS. SWIMMING AND DIVING OFF THE CLIFFS IS NOT RECOMMENDED DUE TO ROCKS, HIGH SURF, CURRENTS AND EVER-PRESENT SHARKS.

KAHAKAI TRAIL PROVIDES PANORAMIC VIEWS OF THE OCEAN BETWEEN KULOA POINT AND THE KĪPAHULU CAMPGROUND. THIS SHORELINE TRAIL EXTENDS A QUARTER-MILE ALONG DRAMATIC CLIFFS.

PIPIWAI TRAIL IS A SOMEWHAT STRENUOUS 4-MILE TRAIL WHICH TAKES HIKERS UPSLOPE ALONG THE PIPIWAI STREAM. ALONG WITH VIEWS OF WATERFALLS, POOLS AND A BAMBOO FOREST, YOU ARE TREATED TO THE SIGHT OF THE REMAINS OF A MILL, DAM AND IRRIGATION FLUMES FROM A SUGAR PLANTATION WHICH EXISTED HERE IN THE 19TH CENTURY. THE TRAIL ENDS NEAR THE BASE OF 400-FOOT WAIMOKU FALLS.

KAPAHU TRAIL, A TRAIL NOW IN THE PLANNING STAGE, WILL TAKE VISITORS TO VIEW KAPAHU FARM.

IT IS VERY IMPORTANT TO RESPECT THE CULTURAL RESOURCES YOU SEE BY STAYING ON THE TRAILS AND NOT DISTURBING FRAGILE SITES.

(TOP) Familiar to all Kīpahulu travelers are the much-photographed **Wailua Falls** (lit. "two waters"), named for two streams flowing into Wailua Cove below. The most attractive of Maui's accessible waterfalls, this 100-foot beauty is viewed through handsome breadfruit leaves from a concrete bridge. A muddy trail leads to the waterfall base, providing a showery exposure to their power. Peer down the chasm below the bridge, but hang onto little hands!

(LEFT) Kīpahulu is not "just around the corner" from Hāna. The **road beyond Hāna** is a slow, bumpy, windy drive (1 to 1.5 hours). Prepare for jiggling stomachs and, during afternoon hours, plenty of traffic. Tiring but scenic, it demands the most driving concentration required yet. If you are tired or running out of time, buy an ice cream in Hāna and turn back. Rental cars are not permitted to drive past Kīpahulu.

(RIGHT) Luxuriance and wildness typify Kīpahulu. All around is brilliantly verdant forest greenery, while at closer quarters, cheery **impatiens** (*Impatiens suttoni*) vie for attention. Native to Madagascar, these bright roadside companions bear fat, elliptical seedpods which children love to pop—hence their alternate name, "touch-me-nots."

(BELOW) **Haleakalā National Park** acts as a focus for visitors and residents in the Kīpahulu area. Enjoy the walking trails, pools, cultural exhibits, maps and Ranger-guided activities. This section of the park is an extension of the dry, volcanic erosional depression (formerly "crater"), accessed from Kahului-side at 10,000-feet elevation.

Photo by Ron Nagata/Haleakalā National Park Service

(ABOVE) Hundreds of cascading pools dot Haleakalā's flanks; **Palikea Stream**, flowing through **'Ohe'o Gulch** (pron. "O-hay-o") is an accessible and especially lovely one. This aerial view shows that Palikea Stream has gouged out about 20 pools within its lowest half-mile, some reachable from the Park's Kūloa Point Trail by stone steps.

(ABOVE) Kīpahulu Valley, an isolated world, extends inland from a broad, coastal lava fan to narrow *pali* (cliffs) on three sides. In early times, groups of extended families shared long triangular, pie-shaped land divisions (*ahupua'a*). Beginning offshore (for fishing), these sections encompassed all elevations, enabling people to obtain all necessary living commodities.

(RIGHT) **Native forest** (note *koa* tree on left) within Kīpahulu Valley. Although part of a Biosphere Reserve, the forest is riddled with wild pigs and increasing numbers of alien shrubs (guava, strawberry guava, purple plague/miconia, African tulip tree, etc.), all requiring constant surveillance and management by State and Federal biologists.

Photo by Ron Nagata/Haleakala National Park Service

(LEFT) One of hundreds of permanent and temporary, unnamed waterfalls plunging off Kīpahulu's inland palisades. **Wailele**, Hawai'i's lovely word for waterfalls (lit. "leaping waters"), have chiseled Maui's basaltic rocks for millennia, and will forever continue their unrelenting sculpture ... always changing.

(LEFT) Whirling furiously through a narrow, meandering gorge, **Pīpīwai Stream** hastens to join Palikea Stream, together gushing to meet the ocean at 'Ohe'o Gulch. Annual rainfall exceeds 200 inches here, so there is usually plenty of water to feed the watercourses, all sculpted deeply through the underlying lava. Right above here are footbridges which allow you to cross the stream and enjoy the spectacular 385-foot high Waimoku Falls.

(TOP & RIGHT) Two views of the famous **'Ohe'o Gulch pools**. In deference to the centuries-old heritage of this picturesque spot and the wishes of the National Park Service and local Hawaiians, please use the traditional gulch name, 'Ohe'o.

(LEFT & BOTTOM LEFT) 'Ohe'o Gulch meets a **stormy sea** on a normal day. It is foolish to swim in the ocean here. Unanticipated flooding and swift, swirling currents are highly dangerous, as are muddied waters and submerged rocks. Avoid being a statistic, do not swim here even on the calmest of days.

(TOP) The National Park Service **Kīpahulu Campground** is 1/8 mile south of the Visitor Center. The campground has picnic tables, BBQ grills, and pit toilets. The Kahakai ("coastal") Trail leads you to 'Ohe'o Gulch. Enjoy Nature: her spectacular, indented coastlines, cascades, pools, sea breezes and rains. No permits are necessary; three days is maximum. Remem-ber about pig-pollution, so bring your own drinking water. WATER IS UNSAFE TO DRINK, causing a variety of disorders ranging from simple diarrhea to serious ghiardiasis and leptospirosis. In this aerial photo, Pipiwai Stream is on the right, Palikea Stream lies to its left; their confluence forms 'Ohe'o Gulch.

(BOTTOM) **Charles Lindbergh**, known to millions for his historic trans-Atlantic flight in 1927, flew in 1974 from a New York hospital to Hāna to spend his last days in solitude with his family. Wracked with incurable cancer, he planned every detail of his simple funeral. A rough-hewn eucalyptus coffin, borne in a local pickup, was his hearse.

(TOP) There is no sign to **Lindbergh's resting place** in a small church graveyard in Kīpahulu. Those who wish to pay him their respects can do as he wished by visiting Kīpahulu, an area he fought to protect.

Photo by Cameron Kepler

(MIDDLE) Heavily wooded, craggy topography abounds here; a jumble of roughly broken slopes sweep ruggedly down to inaccessible sea cliffs. Winding around one valley you pass a white cross, not Lindbergh's, but **Helio's grave**. Born on Maui, Helio Koaeloa (1815–1846) was Maui's first enthusiastic exponent of Catholicism, instructing 4,000 people during his 31 years. DO NOT HIKE THE TRAIL by the information sign; it is treacherous.

Photo by Cameron Kepler

(BOTTOM) Kīpahulu's **old sugar mill**, with its 96-foot high smokestack, reminds us of flourishing, but difficult, times in 1881–1925, when sugar was big business here. Inconveniences galore beset the mill operators: lack of roads and harbors; floods roaring through gullies washing away trails and bridges; and heavy rains muddying up fields and equipment. When sugar died, ranching dominated the area's economy until tourism began in the 1960s. You can still see old railroad tracks from the sugar era on the pier at Hāna Bay.

OUTSTANDING NATIVE PLANTS

Mere mention of Kīpahulu Valley to resident Mauians stirs thoughts of native rain forests harboring rare plants and birds. It is true. Since 1969, Haleakalā National Park has added the wet Kīpahulu District (11,528 acres) to their dry summit region, fully extending the 30,183-acre park from the summit (10,020-feet elevation) to the sea. They have also completed fencing unbelievably difficult sections of the park (to control the ravages of feral pigs), such that upper Kīpahulu Valley still harbors plant, bird and invertebrate rarities. Native flowers: lobelias, begonias and rare greenswords bloom in remote foggy bogs. Such floral specialties are only seen by a handful of hardy biologists and National Park employees willing to be tired, wet and muddy for days on end. There is no access for visitors beyond Waimoku Falls.

(LEFT & RIGHT) A very spiny **native lobelia**, *hāhā nui* (*Cyanea horrida*), closeup and showing its palm-like habit. Shrubby lobelias such as this are true Hawaiian treasures.

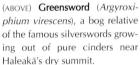

(ABOVE) **Greensword** (*Argyroxiphium virescens*), a bog relative of the famous silverswords growing out of pure cinders near Haleakā's dry summit.

(TOP RIGHT & MIDDLE) A stunning, candelabra-like lobelia, ***koli'i*** (*Trematolobelia macrostachys*) in full bloom and closeup.

(BOTTOM) A **native begonia**, *pu maka nui* (*Hillebrandia sandwicensis*). These large-leaved begonias inhabit shady gullies. Their succulent tissues are eagerly sought and devoured by feral pigs.

ENVIRONMENTAL ALERT

Maui, situated at 21°N latitude in the oceanic subtropics, is an ideal adopted home for introduced tropical plants. Most thrive in gardens and landscaping, presenting few problems. However, some escape into natural or semi-natural ecosystems and literally "run wild." The 1970s/1980s experienced a proliferation of now-familiar pests such as strawberry guava (*Psidium cattleianum*); "inkberry" (*Ardisia elliptica*); yellow, white and *kāhili* gingers (*Hedychium* spp); Java plum (*Syzygium cuminii*); and African tulip tree (*Spathodea campanulata*).

The 1990s ushered in more menacing species, one **so virulent it is capable of *completely and rapidly wiping out Maui's lowland and upland forests.*** This lethal offender is miconia (*Miconia calvescens*), called "purple plague" or "green cancer" in Tahiti, where it has aggressively invaded forests from sea level to 4,260 feet in less than 25 years.

Over 60% of the main island of Tahiti is now dominated by purple plague's thick, dark groves, which grow to 60-feet tall. Today, one quarter of Tahiti's native plant species are nearly extinct. Most of the greenery visible in the accompanying photos is "purple plague," crowding out plants and animals unique to Tahiti.

Despite enormous expenses of time and money, Maui is poised for a similar scenario. Miconia/purple plague is the most serious threat to conservation in Hawai'i (plus feral pigs, of course). Its potential impact is far greater than all other noxious plants combined. Miconia's continuing encroachment into Maui's forests will render all past, present and future conservation efforts futile, since it crowds out all established forms of life. Not even common birds, insects or "tough" plants can survive its onslaught.

Purple plague's horticultural name is velvet leaf (*Miconia calvescens*). In its native tropical America, where it colonizes light gaps, its populations are balanced by natural controls (insects, diseases), absent in Hawai'i. Here, under favorable conditions, a three-foot square experimental plot produced 18,000 seedlings in 6 months! Admittedly attractive, it is esteemed for its large (up to 24-inches long), velvety leaves, shiny green above and bright purple below. Note the three bold leaf veins, a characteristic of its family, *Melastomataceae.**

*Some melastomes *have 5 or 7 bold veins, counting 2 close to the margin. Three, with many ladderlike cross-veins, is more typical.*

WHAT YOU CAN DO: pleas from noxious plant experts

1. Whenever possible, destroy purple plague plants. Look for them while driving around. Report sightings to the State Department of Agriculture, Pest and Weed Control Specialists (phone 871-5656) or Haleakalā National Park (572-4400), or the Maui Invasive Species Committee (573-6472). Look particularly along the Hāna Highway from Huelo to Kīpahulu. Be specific: use stream names (check the concrete bridges) and landmarks (airports, addresses, waterfalls).

2. **No matter how pretty it may be, NEVER buy a purple-flowering bush with prominently 3- or 5-veined leaves.* To do so is a personal contribution to the guaranteed destruction of Maui's rain forests, native biota, watersheds and adjacent coral reefs.** Alert nursery personnel and friends. Already 15 species of *melastomes* grow unchecked in Hawai'i, and almost all are listed as noxious weeds by the State of Hawai'i. These worst offenders on Maui are treated in this book and pictured.

3. Hikers: scrub boots and equipment after hiking anywhere on Maui or on other islands. And don't forget to include your car.

(RIGHT) Miconia/"Purple plague" sapling.

(BELOW) Underside of miconia leaf, showing brilliant purple color and typical ladder-like vein structure.

Photo by Randy Bartlett

121

Top Photos by Art Mediros, Kay Kepler

(RIGHT AND ABOVE) Two views of Tahiti's dramatic interior mountains, now clothed irreparably with purple plague.

(BOTTOM) Glory-bush (*Tibouchina urvilleana*) is a pest in Kōke'e, Kaua'i, and from Volcano to Glenwood, Island of Hawai'i. On Maui, it grows primarily in Kula, where the climate is dry. Should it become a popular garden plant in wetter areas, Maui's forests will suffer irreparably.

ABOUT THE AUTHOR

Dr. Angela Kay Kepler, a naturalized New Zealander, was born in Australia in 1943. A field naturalist, environmental consultant, writer and photographer, she holds degrees from the University of Canterbury (New Zealand), University of Hawai'i (Mānoa Campus) and Cornell University (New York). She also spent one year as a post-doctoral student at Oxford University, England.

Photo by Stewart Pinsky

Angela first came to Hawai'i as an East-West Center foreign student in 1964. Her multi-faceted career involves writing and illustrating natural history books for the "intelligent public," environmental consulting, photography and lecturing on wildlife-oriented eco-tourism ships worldwide.

Over the last 40 years, she has authored or co-authored 17 books, numerous scientific publications and technical reports, written regular newspaper columns on biological and cultural aspects of the Hawaiian Islands and contributed articles and photos to island publications.

An energetic, award-winning photographer, backpacker, birdwatcher, ecologist, adventurer and teacher, she has visited wilderness areas/national parks in nearly 90 countries.

Her extensive ecological and conservation research in Hawai'i, Pacific Islands, Alaska, the Russian Far East and the Caribbean was always focused on the preservation of prime natural areas. Her major project for the past 15 years has been encouraging island governments and cooperating with UNESCO to develop a World Heritage Site encompassing several prime Pacific islands, centered particularly on Millennium Island (due south of Hawai'i).

She recently returned home to Hawai'i after a 14-year absence, and is living on windward Maui, actively involved with landscaping and fruit growing, and in writing a multi-volumed, illustrated guide to fruits in Hawai'i.

OTHER TITLES BY THE AUTHOR

Haleakalā: A Guide to the Mountain with Cameron B. Kepler
The entire mountain, from sun-spangled shorelines through lush lowland forests, verdant pastures and alpine expanses. History, geography, cultural events and accommodations, a complete hiking and camping guide, points of interest, day trips and extended hikes. Over 200 photographs, maps.
ISBN 0-935180-67-2 * 80 pages * 5-3/4" x 8-1/2" * $9.95

Proteas in Hawai'i Photography by Jacob Mau
Floral photography at its best with over 200 photographs on this amazing plant family. A wealth of information on correct English and scientific names including buying and caring for the plants, flower arrangements, general and historic information.
ISBN 0-935180-66-4 * 80 pages * 5-3/4" x 8-1/2" * $9.95

Maui's Hāna Highway: A Visitor's Guide
The incredible 52-mile journey of 617 curves and 56 bridges through some of Hawai'i's most breathtaking scenery. Packed with hundreds of facts and interesting information.
ISBN 0-935180-62-1 * 80 pages * 5-3/4" x 8-1/2" * $9.95

Exotic Tropicals of Hawai'i: Heliconias, Anthuriums, Gingers and Decorative Foliage Photography by Jacob Mau
A complete account of over 136 species of Hawai'i's well-known, as well as lesser-known tropicals, including birds-of-paradise, ornamental bananas, fanciful and "jungle" foliage. Correct English and scientific names, usage, flower arrangement.
ISBN 0-935180-83-4 * 112 pages * 5-3/4" x 8-1/2" * $9.95

Sunny South Maui
An exploration of Maui's south coastal plains—an area rich in history and nature as well as man-made environs. From Kahului to La Perousse, including Molokini Islet and Kaho'olawe.
ISBN 1-56647-012-9 * 144 pages * 6" x 9" * softcover * $14.95

Majestic Moloka'i: A Nature Lover's Guide with Cameron B. Kepler

A pictorial description of Moloka'i and its many natural wonders. A conservation message permeates the text, which also includes an appreciation of the ways of the early Hawaiians.

ISBN 0-935180-73-7 * 144 pages * 6" x 9" * softcover * $14.95

Wonderful West Maui

Over 250 color photographs capture the magic and splendor of West Maui, revealing its many wondrous sights: iridescent foothills, rainbows, glorious beaches, precipitous mountains, natural life, cloud patterns. Included are verdant 'Īao Valley, historic Lāhainā town, remote rain forests, steep inland valleys, as well as photos of sites accessible only to the most experienced hikers.

ISBN 1-56647-013-7 * 146 pages * 6" x 9" * softcover * $14.95

INDEX